CASINO GAMING DICTIONARY
Terms and Language
For Managers

George G. Fenich
Kathryn Hashimoto

KENDALL/HUNT PUBLISHING COMPANY
4050 Westmark Drive   Dubuque, Iowa 52002

P9-DTL-381

ACKNOWLEDGEMENTS

Of our spouses (they know why).
Of our mothers,
Mitsuyo Hashimoto Akiba
Mary Kaputa Fenich

Copyright © 1996 by Kendall/Hunt Publishing Company

ISBN 0-7872-1235-0

Printed in the United States of America
10 9 8 7 6 5 4 3 2 1

ABOUT THIS BOOK

The casino gaming industry is experiencing exponential expansion with educators, researchers, policy analysts, students, and the general public showing increasing fascination with the subject. However, attempting to read and find out more about casino gaming can be as frustrating as trying to understand a menu in a French restaurant. Many of the words and phrases seem to be in a foreign language: so too is the language of the casino gaming industry with jargon and business buzz words making comprehension difficult.

This book solves the problem by defining the terms and language of casino management. Over 1,500 terms and phrases, with unique uses or applications in the casino industry, are defined and explained. This is one of the most extensive compilations of terms used in this industry, but it goes a step further than other glossaries and dictionaries by including:
> names of the most popular games and how they are
>> played;
> gambling jargon;
> phrases used by dealers when referring to both their bosses
>> and their customers;
> types of cheating techniques;
> and <u>most importantly,</u>
> the common terms and phrases used by managers in the
>> casino departments of

marketing	accounting	economics
finance	management	hotels/restaurants

No one with any interest, whether it be casual or serious, in the casino gaming industry can afford to be without this valuable resource.

ABOUT THE AUTHORS

Georeg G. Fenich, Ph.D. spent over fifteen years as a hospitality industry practitioner before joining the faculty of the School of Hotel, Restaurant, and Tourism Management at Fairleigh Dickinson University, where he is an Associate Professor. George has done extensive research on the casino industry including work for the Casino Association of New Jersey. The results have been disseminated in working papers, academic journals, and conferneces. He was instrumental in putting toegther the college text "Casino Management for the 90's." Along with Kathryn Hashimoto, he helped establish the Casino Gaming SIS for CHRIE.

George G. Fenich has served hospitality education in many ways including: as a founder and Commissioner of the Accreditation Commission for Programs in Hospitality Administration; as an officer and President of the Hospitality Educators of the Middle Atlantic Region; and as a member of the Board of Directors of the Council on Hotel, Restaurant, and Institutional Education.

Kathryn Hashimoto, Ph.D. worked in the hospitality industry for over ten years doing marketing and sales. An additional nine years were spent as a professor of marketing, in business programs. During this time, she became interested in gaming and presented several papers on casinos. In order to develop a better understanding of casinos, she studied to become a dealer in Atlantic City and organized a special instest section on gaming for CHRIE. She worked with Dr. Fenich on "Casino Management for the 90's."

To continue her research on gaming and to increase access to casino information, Kathy helped form the Asscoiation for Casino Education (A.C.E.), a non-profit organization. It was created to disseminate information about the casino industry to educators and researchers, and to act as a link between industry and education.

-A-

ABANDON - to relinquish a hand or deal.

ABOVE - a casino's earnings as recorded in its bookkeeping ledger.

ABSOLUTE ADVANTAGE - term in economics which refers to the ability of one firm to produce a good or service more efficiently than another.

ACCOUNTABILITY - a persons ability to carry out assigned responsibilities and to be answerable for decisions.

ACCOUNT PAYABLE - an amount owed by the business.

ACCOUNT RECEIVABLE - an amount owed to the business.

ACE - 1) a playing card, 2) in blackjack, playing card with a value of one or eleven, 3) in craps, a single dot on one die, 4) one dollar bill.

A CHEVAL - in roulette, a bet on two numbers adjacent on the layout.

ACROSS THE BOARD - in racing, when a better places wagers on win, place, and show.

ACTION - sum total of all wagers made or all gambling activity.

ACTIVE PLAYER - in baccarat, a player who represents a combined group of players in wagering against the bank.

ADA - abbreviation for the Americans with Disabilities Act.

ADDICTION - a physiological and/or psychological dependency on goods or services.

ADMINISTRATIVE PRINCIPLES - a branch of classical management theory concerned with identified principles of planning, organizing, commanding, coordinating, and controlling in an effort to manage the entire organization.

ADVERTISING - any paid, non-personal communication transmitted through mass media by an identified sponsor.

AFFIRMATIVE ACTION PROGRAMS - in a company, an agenda that enhances the organizational status of members of protected groups, i.e. minorities.

AFRICAN DOMINOES - dice.

AGENT - 1) an accomplice of a casino employee who poses as a player as part of a scheme to defraud the casino, 2) person who takes lottery or numbers bets.

AGGREGATE DEMAND - economic term referring to the total spending in a region as a whole over a given time frame, as in "the aggregate demand for gambling in Atlantic City is one billion dollars."

AMERICAN PLAN or AP - a billing arrangement in a lodging establishment under which room charges include the guestroom and three meals per day.

AMERICANS WITH DISABILITIES ACT - federal legislation passed in the nineteen-nineties that requires public spaces, including casinos, to be accessible and/or user friendly to people with handicaps.

AMERICAN ROULETTE - roulette wheel with two zeros, 0 and 00, with alternating black and red numbers that follow and ordered and symmetrical pattern with each odd number exactly opposite the next higher even number.

AMORTIZATION - in accounting, a product cost that is written off on or paid down, over a period of time longer than a year.

ANCHOR MAN - in blackjack, the last player who is to the immediate right of the dealer.

ANCHOR SLOT - in blackjack, the player in the first position, the same as first base.

ANTE - in a card game, a wager placed before the first card is dealt.

ANY - in craps, the "any craps" wager.

APRON - place on the roulette table where chips are stored, not in a tray.

ARM - a gambling operation backed or under the protection of organized crime as in "the arm."

AROUND THE CORNER - a protocol in cards where the ace is permitted to link the lowest and highest cards in a sequence such as queen, king, ace, deuce, two, etc.

ARRIVAL DATE - in lodging, the day a guest plans to appear with the expectation of a room being available for them.

ASSETS - anything a business owns that has monetary value.

ATMOSPHERE - the interior of a facility, decor, or atmosphere that is used to develop an image, differentiate the facility from its competitors, and draw customers.

ATMOSPHERICS - a consumer behavior term that refers to the use of space and physical features in a design to evoke certain effect in buyers.

ATTACK - gambler bets against the bank.

ATTITUDES or OPINIONS - the positive, neutral, or negative feelings a person has about macro issues such as a company, institution, goods, services, the economy, politics, etc.

AUCTION - in chemin de fer, the bidding to decide who will be the banker.

AUTHORITY - the right to take action and utilize business resources.

AUTOCRATIC LEADER - someone who relies upon direct commands and use of position authority as a management style with little input from others.

AUTONOMY - the degree to which the job allows individual freedom, independence, and discretion in such activities as scheduling work and determining task procedures.

AVERAGE DAILY RATE or ADR - in lodging, the occupancy ratio derived by dividing rooms revenue by the number of rooms sold.

AX - 1) when an employee is terminated or fired, 2) when the house takes its cut.

AUDITION - 1) a try out, 2) to deal for a supervisor with the hope of obtaining a job.

-B-

BACCARAT - card game made famous by James Bond in which players bet against the player who is the banker and a shoe is used to deal the cards, typically a high stakes game. Also called Chemin de fer, Nevada Baccarat, Punto Banco, or American Baccarat.

BACCARAT BANQUE - a version of baccarat found predominantly in France where the casino dealer acts as the banker, deals all cards, and banks all bets. Cards are dealt to two different players, each on either side of the table.

BACK COUNTING - when someone who is not playing the table counts cards or counts down the deck. When a favorable count occurs, the back counter places their wager, and is usually done from a place behind the actual players at the blackjack table.

BACKER MAN - also called the bankroller, it is the backer who finances a game.

BACK LINE - the "Don't Pass" line.

BACK LINE ODDS - with a bet on the "Don't Pass" line, a craps player lays the odds on the point number.

BACK OF THE HOUSE - the functional areas of the casino, hotel, or restaurant in which personnel have little or no direct contact with the guests.

BACK TO BACK - winning two hands in a row.

BAD DEBT - in accounting, the amount of money owed to the firm that is written off because it is uncollectable.

BADGE - slang term for a gaming enforcement officer or a police officer.

BAD PAPER - in accounting, checks that are not honored at the bank.

BAGGAGE - 1) a person who frequents a game but does not play, 2) a person who cannot pay their own expenses and expects someone else to do so.

BAGGED - arrested.

4

BALANCE SHEET - financial statement identifying the assets and liabilities of an organization at a specific point in time.

BALL - the round, sphere shaped object made to rigid standards of density and composition, that is spun around the roulette wheel and, subsequently, falls into the winning slot number and color.

BALL OUT - when the ball (see above) bursts out of the roulette wheel, invalidating the spin.

BANANAS - twenty dollar chips that are used in baccarat that are yellow in color.

BANCO - 1) used in baccarat when a player wants to challenge the bank, 2) term for the bank in chemin de fer, 3) old time cheating scheme.

BANCO SUIVI - in baccarat, a call by a player after they have lost a coup, done when he wants to bet against the bank again.

BANG UP - closing the game or the house upon command from a boss or supervisor.

BANK - 1) sum of money present at a gambling table also called the bankroll, 2) house or dealer who pays off, 3) starting quantity of chips at the table.

BANK CRAPS - one version of craps where the players wager against the house or banker and not against each other.

BANK HAND - one of two betting positions in baccarat.

BANKING GAME - any casino game where players bet against the house rather than each other.

BANKROLL - in casinos, the amount of money the table is stocked with at the beginning of the shift.

BANKROLL MAN - the financier of a game.

BAR - 1) as in "to bar," not allowed. Barring twelve or two on "don't pass" bets allows the casino to accept don't bets, 2) area where alcoholic beverages are served.

BARBER POLE - a wager consisting of chips of various denominations and, thus, colors. When such a wager wins, chips are divided by color and paid by color.

BARRIERS TO COMPETITION - factors that reduce the amount of competition or the number of firms, thereby allowing greater economic concentration to occur. Examples of barriers include legal barriers and regulatory barriers.

BASIC STRATEGY - 1) elementary or not advanced approach to trying to win at a game, 2) basic approach used by card counters where memory in counting down the deck is not used.

BEAN - a low value or one dollar chip.

BEAN COUNTER - an accountant.

BEANSHOOTER - a cheating technique where a simple holdout device is worn on the arm.

BEAT - 1) to overcome or beat the odds, 2) to cheat someone out of money in a gambling game.

BEEF - an argument or complaint from a player against another player or the house.

BEEFER - complaining player.

BELIEFS - people's ideas about the world around them and how it operates.

BELLY STRIPPERS - cards that have been trimmed so that some of them are wider at the center along the sides than at the ends.

BENCHMARKING - in business, the search for the best practices among competitors or non-competitors that lead to their superior performance.

BENDER - in cheating, a person who puts a very slight bend on the corners of cards he may want later.

BENJI - a one hundred dollar bill.

BENNY BLUE - in craps, a seven out.

BERNOULLI SYSTEM - a closed mathematical system where each outcome has a constant probability of coming up, from one trial to another, the results of each trial are mutually exclusive of each other, each trial is independent of the other, and the sum of all possible outcomes is one hundred percent, such as in dice or roulette.

BERNOULLI THEOREM - the canon that puts forth that the larger the number of trials within a system, the greater the likelihood that the actual results will approximate their mathematical expectation.

BEST OF IT - when one player has a greater likelihood of winning than the other players, due to a mathematical edge, greater skill, or through cheating.

BET - wager made by the player in the casino.

BET BLIND - a wager made without looking at one's cards.

BET THE POT - a wager that matches the amount already on the table or in the kitty.

BET BOTH WAYS - where the table has two-way action, betting on either the right or the wrong.

BET THE DICE TO WIN - betting right that the shooter will pass.

BET THE LIMIT - wagering the maximum amount that the table rules or the house allows.

BETTING RATIO - the mathematical relationship between the highest and lowest wager placed by a player.

BETTING RIGHT - in craps, a wager that the shooter will win.

BETTING SYSTEM - a series of mathematical rules that determine how a player should allocate his money between wagers on different trials in a game.

BETTING TRUE COUNT - varying bets based on the count, higher for "plus counts" and lower for "minus counts."

BETTING WRONG - in craps, a wager that the shooter will lose.

BEVEL, BEVELED - when dice have been modified such that one or more sides are slightly rounded rather than flat, so that the dice tend to fall on a certain number, thus improving the players odds. Beveled dice are illegal.

BICYCLE - a card style.

BIG BERTHA - in slots, oversized machines.

BIG CON - any elaborate con game or scheme lasting over several days and involving numerous people.

BIG DICK - in craps, the point ten.

BIG 6 OR 8 - in craps, wagering that either six or eight will come up before seven and pays one to one.

BIG ORDER - bookmakers phrase for a large bet.

BIG SIX - game that uses a large, vertical wheel with varied payoffs, often called the Wheel of Fortune or Money Wheel.

BIG STORE - a fictitious establishment used in the big con and can include a gambling house, brokerage house, or bookmaking place, where the mark is led to believe he is going to swindle.

BILL - a gambler's term for a one hundred dollar note as in "I lost five bills yesterday."

BINGO - game where the goal is to match the numbers on a playing card to those drawn by the house using numbered balls. The standard winning pattern on the card is a complete list or line of numbers in a horizontal, vertical, or diagonal pattern. The game is a mainstay of Native American Casinos, and is not played in Atlantic City.

BIRD - a loser or sucker who appears to enjoy giving their money away.

BITE - A request for a loan or credit, as in "to put the bite on someone."

BLACK - in roulette, a bet paying one to one.

BLACKBOOK - 1) a document put out by the Nevada Gaming Commission with the names and pictures of mobsters. If a casino allows entry of anyone listed, they can lose their gaming license, 2) pictures and names of over twenty-five hundred undesirables developed by an ex-lawman from Nevada, 3) book of clients and their preferences kept by a prostitute.

BLACKJACK - 1) card game whose object is to collect cards that score twenty one or less, 2) a hand comprised of an ace and a ten, or court card, valued at ten, to give a two card total of twenty-one, and a natural winner, but cannot be formed after splitting two aces, 3) what you have when you beat the dealer, also called "BJ."

BLACK LINE WORK - a cheating method in cards where a small cut is made along the black line that borders each picture on a face card, and is felt by the cheat as a means of identifying the card.

BLACKLIST - list and/or photographs of certain people who are not allowed in the casino.

BLACK OUT WORK - a cheating technique in cards where the cards are marked by blocking out some of the design with white ink or some element of the design is somewhat embellished.

BLACKS - one hundred dollar chips, usually black in color.

BLISTER - a cheating methods in cards where a small bump is placed on the back of a card so the cheat can identify it whenever it is on the top of the deck.

BLOCK - in lodging, a number of rooms set aside for members of a group, such as gamblers with comps.

BLOW - 1) to lose, 2) to be caught in the act of cheating.

BLUEPRINT - a precise schematic diagram of a building, or part of a building, where nonessential elements are eliminated, thus conveying information about the size, relative position, and distance of various parts.

BLUFF - in poker, to bet heavily in spite of holding a weak hand in an attempt to make one's opponents think a good hand is held, with the expectation that opponents will drop out, allowing the bluffer to win.

BOARDS - 1) the raised element surrounding the table also called the rail or the blackboard, 2) in Atlantic City refers to the boardwalk when a player decides it is time to leave, 3) group or commission that deals with policy issues occurring at the highest level of an organization such as the Gaming Board.

BOAT - receptacle that contains the unused dice.

BODY LANGUAGE - non-verbal body expressions that act as messages or impart additional information about the person or the verbal message.

BOND - 1) in human resources, the affiliation between organization members, 2) in finance, an interest bearing certificate issued by a corporation or government, promising to pay interest and to repay a sum of money (the principal) at a specified date in the future.

BONES - dice.

BOOK, BOOKIE, BOOKMAKER - 1) the person who collects and pays off bets for the house, both in and out of a casino, 2) an establishment or individual that accepts wagers on the outcome of races and sporting events, as in "Sports Book."

BOOK - in lodging, to sell or reserve rooms ahead of time, i.e. before the arrival date.

BOP - when a player jumps from table to table, often done in conjunction with partners at various tables who are card counters.

BOTTOM DEALER - a cheating technique where the dealer draws cards from the bottom of the deck.

BOULEUR - croupier who spins the roulette wheel.

BOUNCER - 1) employee who is usually burly, keeps order in the house or bar, and ejects trouble making patrons, 2) a check that cannot be collected.

BOWL - in roulette, the wooden recess that holds the spinning part of the wheel.

BOX - 1) in craps, the receptacle or bowl where the stick man keeps the dice, 2) in blackjack, a square area on the table in front of the player in which the bet is usually placed.

BOXCARS - in craps, to roll the number twelve.

BOXMAN or BOXPERSON - casino employee in charge of the craps table who supervises the stick man or dealer; is subordinate to the floorman and pit boss; who deposits money in the drop box; and monitors the payouts to ensure accuracy.

BOX UP or BOX THEM UP - act of mixing the dice by the stickman so that the player may select another pair.

BOYS - 1) in craps, the dealers, 2) players, gamblers, 3) members of organized crime.

BP - short hand for big player or high roller.

BRAINSTORMING - in organizations, an idea generating process that encourages alternatives while withholding criticism.

BRASS BUTTONS - same origin as'"cop", meaning a police officer.

BREAK or BROKE - 1) a hand in blackjack that exceeds twenty-one, 2) rest period for dealers, usually fifteen to twenty minutes in each hour worked.

BREAK A GAME - when one or more players ends a game by winning either, all the money at a particular table, or all the money the casino has.

BREAK EVEN - to win as much as ones loses.

BREAK EVEN ANALYSIS - a managerial control aid that provides information on the required number of units or sales volume at which the business neither makes nor loses money.

BREAK IN - to get a dealer's job with little or no prior experience, new or novice dealer.

BREAK IT DOWN - to cut chips into countable stacks or to segregate them by color.

BREAKS - luck, either good or bad, as in "those are the breaks."

BREAK THE DECK - in blackjack, to reshuffle the cards, usually in an effort to foil a card counter.

BREAK THE BANK - in European table games, the casino imposes a limit on the amount of casino chips supplied to each table. When the table loses its "bank", it shuts down.

BRICK - in craps, a cheating technique where a die has been cut so that it is not true, same as flat.

BRIDGE - in cheating, to slightly bend the ten-cards lengthwise so that they are easy to spot on the table or in the deck.

BROKE MONEY - a gift from the house of carfare or transportation costs to a player who lost all their money, also referred to as a "ding."

BRAND LOYALTY - a pattern of repeat product purchases or uses, accompanied by an underlying positive attitude toward the brand, as in someone who always goes to Harrah's Casinos.

BRUSH or THE BRUSH - 1) a cheating method in cards where the perpetrator exchanges one of the cards in his hand for one from his accomplices hand in the act of pushing the other player's cards aside on the table, 2) a cheating method in craps where the cheat exchanges one pair of dice for another in the act of pushing the dice aside on the table.

BUCK - 1) one dollar bill, 2) machismo male.

BUCK THE GAME - bet against the house.

BUDGET - guides the allocation of financial, human, and physical resources, often used in planning and control.

BUFFET - in restaurants, a method of service where the guest serves themselves, includes a wide variety of items, and is the "meal comp" provided to low rollers.

BUG - a device placed under the table or on the slot machine as a means of cheating.

BUILDUP - a scam which causes the cashier to return too much money in making change for a large bill.

BULL - detective or police officer.

BULLET - ace card.

BUM MOVE - suspicious action by a player.

BUMP INTO - an action by the dealer where he pushes a stack of chips next to and touching a shorter stack, and removes the excess to make both stacks equal.

BUM STEER - incorrect or bad information.

BUNDLE - large bankroll, much money.

BUREAUCRACY - a system or organization and management characterized by specialization, a well defined hierarchy, and rules, impersonal regulations, and fixed criteria for promotion and selection, such as in government.

BURN A CARD, BURNED CARDS - 1) removing one or more cards from the top of a deck and placing them, face up, on the bottom, often done in blackjack or poker after the cards are shuffled, 2) after cards which have been shuffled are put into the shoe, some of the first cards to come up are discarded.

BURNED OUT - 1) when a cheating method becomes so well known as to be useless, 2) individual condition resulting from extended periods of stress and pressure.

BURNT CARD - in single deck blackjack, a card that is reversed on the bottom of the deck, to conceal it.

BURN UP - 1) an angry person, 2) said of dice when they are making money passes.

BURST - 1) in blackjack, cards totaling more than twenty one, 2) bust, break.

BUST - 1) in blackjack, cards totaling more than twenty one, 2) burst, break, worthless hand.

BUST CARD - in blackjack, the nomenclature for the two, three, four, five, or six as the dealer's upcard, because it is a difficult point to hit.

BUST HAND - in blackjack, a hand totaling from twelve to sixteen and also called a hard hand.

BUSTERS - mis-spotted dice.

BUST-OUT MAN - a cheater who specializes in switching crooked dice.

BUTTERFLY CUP - a dice cup that is modified in a way that allows the cheat to switch dice in the process of shaking them prior to rolling.

BUTTONS - 1) in roulette, the small markers used to identify the temporary value of a player's chips, 2) in craps, the small markers used to identify different types of bets, 3) small markers used to record the amount of chips taken form a table without being paid for in cash or other chips.

BUY BET - in craps, a bet made on a point number, betting that the number will be rolled before a seven, with the bet usually bought at a premium of five percent of the amount of the bet and paid at true odds.

BUY BEHIND - in craps, to purchase true odds behind a point number, wagering that the number will not be rolled before a seven, at a premium of five percent.

BUY IN - in poker, the sum of money a player exchanges for chips and also called "buying in."

-C-

C&E - in craps, a split bet covering any craps and eleven.

CACKLE - in craps, to feign the shaking of dice when, in reality, they are under control.

CAGE - location of the casino cashier.

CALCULATORS - mathematicians, or odds men, who work in the calculations room at the racetrack.

CALL - 1) the announcement of colors, numbers, changes, and wagers, 2) in poker, to end betting on a hand by covering the last gambler's wager without raising it.

CALL BET - a verbal wager that is made known by players and is illegal in New Jersey.

CALLER - in keno or bingo, the person who runs the game by handling the numbers and calling out or posting those selected.

14

CALL MAN - casino employee who runs the baccarat game.

CALL PLAYS - in blackjack, used by teams of card counters. Verbal signal to the player of the team by the counter of the team, how much to bet and how to play the hand.

CANE - in craps, the curved stick used by the stickman to reclaim the dice after each throw.

CAN'T GET TO HIM - someone who is not tempted by a bribe.

CAPABLE - used in reference to a card or dice mechanic who does a good job of cheating.

CAPACITY PLANNING - a determination of the space needed to hold a given number of people or players.

CAPITAL - 1) in finance, money needed for development, 2) gambler's available money.

CAPITAL EXPENDITURES - a business' expenditures that are long term investments in fixed assets such as a buildings.

CAPPED DICE - a cheating technique in craps where the dice have been modified so that some sides are more rubbery or softer than others and which favor certain numbers.

CAPPING BETS - 1) when the dealer pays off a bet by placing the payoff on top of the original wager, 2) illegally adding chips to a wager after the game is in progress.

CARD COUNTERS - intensely businesslike players who closely track which cards have been dealt and adjust the size of their bets to reflect the extent to which the remaining cards are favorable to them.

CARD - 1) basic device for many table games including baccarat, blackjack, and poker consisting of a stack or deck of fifty-two, made of laminated paper, and being numbered on one side with a design on the other, 2) a funny person.

CARD DOWN - expression directed to a floorperson to indicate that a card has fallen off the table.

CAROUSEL - in a casino, the island of slot machines with one or more attendants in the middle.

CARPET JOINT - a plush casino catering to high rollers.

CARRE or SQUARE BET- in roulette, a bet on four numbers whose boxes form a square on the table.

CARRY A SLUG - a cheating technique when a deck is shuffled without disturbing a particular group of cards, usually on the top or bottom.

CARTE BLANCHE - 1) a player who has unlimited credit, 2) a hand of cards that contains no face cards.

CARTWHEEL - a silver dollar.

CASE BET - a wager that includes all the money or chips that a player has left.

CASE STUFF - any cheating method that is not very well known, even among professionals.

CASH BANK - an amount of money given to a cashier or server at the start of each workshift so that they can handle the various transactions that occur. This person is responsible for the cash bank and for all cash, checks, or other negotiable instruments received during the workshift.

CASH BUDGETS - financial aid which contains estimates of cash receipts and cash expenditures for a period of time.

CASH COW - a product or service that has a dominant position or a sizable market but limited growth potential, and which a company often uses as a cash subsidy for other products.

CASH FLOW - relates the amount and timing of revenues received, to the amount and timing of expenditures made during, a specific time period.

CASHIER - the casino employee who handles transactions in the cage.

CASHIERS CAGE - the place in the casino where transactions with players take place, is highly controlled, and where the cashier works.

CASH OUT - changing chips for currency.

CASING - checking out or scouting the casino in preparation for some illegal activity, such as cheating or theft.

CASINO - establishment where betting is allowed and is legal which may or may not contain other amenities such as bars, food service, lodging, etc. Also called house, joint, shop, store, toilet, trap.

CASINO ADMINISTRATOR - person responsible for the policies and procedures of the casino.

CASINO HOTEL - a lodging facility that also contains gambling.

CASINO MANAGER - top person in the casino.

CASINO SUPERVISOR - casino employee responsible for overseeing one or more table games and can include floorpersons and pit bosses.

CATCH - for a casino employee to do, get, or pull.

CATCHES - the numbers picked by a gambler which come up on the casino boards.

CATWALK - concealed area, usually a walkway, above the casino floor used for observing play on the casino floor and where the objective is security.

CAUGHT UP - when management determines that a player owes money and cannot pay it, thus no longer has credit, as in "they caught up with him."

CENTER DEALING - a cheating technique where cards are dealt from the middle of the deck.

CENTER FIELD - 1) in blackjack, the center box or position, directly across from the dealer, 2) in craps, the field bet nine.

CENTRAL BUSINESS DISTRICT or CBD - the hub of business activity in a community which includes offices and retailing.

CENTRALIZATION - in business management, the extent to which decision authority and responsibility rests with few, rather than many, organizational members, usually higher-level managers.

CENTRAL LIMIT THEOREM - the statistical rule that, as the sample size is increased, so the sampling distribution approaches the normal distribution form and serves as the basis for craps.

CENTRAL PROCESSING UNIT OR CPU - a phase computing system in which data is processed based upon programmed instructions.

CENTURY - one hundred dollars.

CHAIN OF COMMAND - in management, an unbroken hierarchy of authority linking superiors and subordinates in an organization.

CHANCE - statistical probability.

CHANGE AGENTS - 1) on the casino floor, those who exchange cash as a service to players, 2) in an organization, people who act as catalysts and manage the change process.

CHANGE COLORS - to exchange one denomination of casino chips for another, thus changing the color of ones chips.

CHANGE UP or COLOR UP - to change one denomination of chips for the next higher denomination, thus substituting colors.

CHANNEL - the medium though which a message travels.

CHARISMATIC LEADERSHIP - followers make attributions of heroic or extraordinary leadership abilities when they observe certain behaviors in these mangers or owners, and often attributed to the movers and shakers in the casino industry.

CHARTER BUS - in casinos, the bus program the casino/hotel arranges or leases.

CHEAT - bottom dealer, also called a mechanic.

CHECK DOWN - expression directed to a floorperson when a chip or money drops to the floor .

CHECKER - casino employee who monitors the shills to determine how many players they bring to the game.

CHECK, CHECKS - casino chips which are non-metallic gaming tokens that are used in place of currency in the casino and come in various denominations ranging from one to five thousand dollars:

$1.00	white
$2.50	pink
$5.00	red
$20.00	yellow
$25.00	green
$100.00	black
$500.00	purple
$1,000.00	orange
$5,000.00	gray

CHECK COP - a cheating technique where adhesive paste is put on the palm of the hand and, when the palm is placed over a stack of chips, the top one adheres to the palm and is stolen.

CHECK COPPING - stealing chips off the table, either from other players or the pot.

CHECK OUT - 1) to observe or analyze something or someone, 2) in lodging, the procedures involved in the departure of a guest from the property, including settlement of the guest's account.

CHIEF EXECUTIVE OFFICER or CEO - the highest, top-level, manager in an organization.

CHIEF INFORMATION OFFICER or CIO - a senior level manager whose major role is to oversee information as a resource in strategic, tactical, and operational planning.

CHEMIN DE FER - a form of baccarat where the players compete among themselves and not against the house, common in Nevada.

CHICKEN FEED - an insignificant quantity of money, small change.

CHILL - to lose interest.

CHIP CUP - a cheating technique that uses a stack of simulated chips which is actually a hollow cup and is used to steal chips from the casino.

CHIPPY - 1) an inexperienced player, 2) a sucker.

CHIPS - 1) tokens used instead of cash on all gaming tables and used to mark a bet, 2) a gambler with a lot of money, 3) the small electronic device which is actually etched silicon in a slot machine that contains the computer program.

CHUCK A LUCK - a game of chance where three dice are spun in an hour glass shaped wire frame called a chuck cage and a betting layout. Also called Nevada Chuck-a-luck, Grand Hazard, or Hazard.

CHUMP - a sucker, chippy, mark, monkey, pheasant, bird, or greenie.

CHUNK - to regularly make large bets, or too large a bet.

CIRCLED GAME - situation where the sports book reduces the normal betting limit on a game.

CLAIM BET ARTIST - in cheating, a person who generally claims bets around dice tables, where players can lose track of their bets.

CLAIMER or COLLECTOR - in a slot cheating scam, the person who has responsibility for collecting the jackpot.

CLAPPER - the item that hangs in a vertical position at the top of the big six wheel, is often made of leather, rides on the top of the pegs, and when the wheel stops determines the winning number.

CLASSICAL DECISION MODEL - in economics, a decision making approach that assumes individuals make decisions based on rational and unemotional thinking.

CLEAN - to take all of the money a player has.

CLEAN MOVE - a well executed cheating action.

CLEAN HAND - an empty hand which can be shown not to contain palmed cards or dice.

CLEAR - 1) not guilty of cheating, 2) free of debt.

CLERK - 1) very good dealer, 2) any dealer.

CLIP - cheat.

CLOCK IN - when a casino employee who is paid on an hourly basis arrives at work or departs and has his time slip record the hour.

CLOCKING - keeping track of action such as the number of hands dealt or the number of spins taken on a big six wheel during a given time period.

CLOSED CARDS - cards dealt face down.

CLOSER - the form left in the tray at closing which designates the value of the tray or inventory.

C-NOTE - one hundred dollar bill.

COCKED DICE - in craps, when one or more dice stop on some surface other than the felt and, thus lie at an angle which makes it hard to determine which die surface is pointing up.

COERCIVE POWER - in management, the ability of a leader to administer punishment to subordinates, thus gaining power through fear.

COGNETTE - in baccarat, a slot in the table reserved for the bank's winnings or cut of winnings.

COHESIVENESS - in groups, particularly certain departments of a business, the strength of interpersonal attraction between members and the degree to which they are motivated to remain part of the group.

COLD DECK - 1) a deck or shoe unfavorable to the player, 2) a cheating technique where the deck of cards has been arranged in a certain order for purposes of switching later for the deck in play.

COLD DICE - dice that are not making the player's point.

COLD PLAYER - a gambler who is on a losing streak or a run of bad luck.

COLLECTIVE BARGAINING - process for negotiating a union contract and for administering the contract after it has been negotiated.

21

COLLUSION - 1) cooperation between two individuals for mutual gain, 2) agreement between different firms to cooperate by rasing prices, dividing markets, or otherwise restraining competition.

COLOR - designation of the value of chips by their color.

COLOR FOR COLOR - expression used by dealers when they pay out a bet by matching each denomination of chip wagered.

COMBINATION BET - in roulette, a bet on more than one number, using a single chip.

COMBINATIONS - syndicate of gamblers.

COME BET - in craps, the same as a pass line wager.

COME OUT ROLL - in craps, the first roll after a pass line decision which establishes the point.

COME UP - a chance or number comes up, when it wins.

COMING IN ONE HIGH - a cheating technique used by a dealer to short a player on the payoff by secretly transferring a chip from the player's wager to the payoff stack.

COMING OUT - in craps, when the stickman informs the players that the dice are ready to be thrown which is a warning that all bets must be placed immediately.

COMMISSION - a percentage or fee charged by the casino on some bets or games and monitored by the dealer using plastic markers or lammers placed in a specific area of the layout that corresponds to the player's numbered seats. In baccarat it is five percent.

COMPENSATION - all of the direct and indirect pay that an employee receives for the job performed.

COMPETITIVE ADVANTAGE - a term used in economics to describe the distinct competency one entity has over its competitors. These competitors can include business', communities, regions, etc.

COMPARATIVE ADVANTAGE - an economic term that says a firm, nation, or region should specialize in producing commodities that it can produce at relatively lower costs than others.

COMPS - short for complimentary goods or services given to players and can apply to things as low cost as drinks to full room, beverage, and transportation costs. They are a marketing tool used to attract players to a certain casino and are also called full compos (rooms, food, beverage).

CONCIERGE - an employee whose basic task is to serve as the guest's liaison with both hotel and non-hotel attractions, facilities, services, and activities.

CONFLICT - perceived incompatible differences that results in interference or opposition.

CONNECTED - having association with organized crime.

CONSPICUOUS CONSUMPTION - the purchase and prominent display of luxury goods to provide evidence of a consumer's ability to afford them and often attributed to high rollers.

CONSUMER BEHAVIOR - the process where individuals decide whether, what, when, where, how, and from whom to purchase goods and services.

CONTENT THEORIES - theories developed by Maslow and Hertzberg that describe the various factors, or content, that effect human motivation.

CONTINENTAL BREAKFAST - a small meal which usually includes a beverage, rolls, butter, and jam or marmalade.

CONTINGENCY PLANS - in management, predesigned actions for meeting certain possible conditions.

CONTROL - the process of monitoring activities to ensure they are being accomplished as planned and of correcting any significant deviations.

C.O.O. - short for chief operating officer.

COOLER - a prestacked deck that is secretly switched for the deck in play.

COP - 1) to get, take, or steal, 2) to win a bet.

CORE VALUES - a set of important values that seem to define a specific culture and is important with regards to how society views gambling.

CORKER - an unusual player, can mean good or bad.

CORNER BET - in roulette, a wager placed on the intersection of four numbers that is paid at eight to one and is also called a square bet.

CORPORATION - a business firm formally incorporated under state law which, thus, separates the company from its owners or stockholders and also limits owners' liability.

CORRELATION ANALYSIS - a statistical process that estimates to what extent variables are related to one another.

COUNT - 1) the act of tallying the chips in a tray or the proceeds from a drop box, 2) the cumulative value of all cards played at any given time.

COUNT DOWN - an action by a dealer to make small, regulation sized, stacks of chips from taller ones, so that they can be more easily counted from a distance.

COUNTER - in blackjack, a card counter.

COUNTER CHECK - a draft used to secure credit or markers.

COUP - In European casinos, the term for a complete round of play in such games as baccarat or roulette.

COURT CARDS - the jack, queen, or king, all of which have a value of ten in blackjack and zero in baccarat.

COWBOY - a fast or brash gambler.

COVER - 1) to place a wager on a table, 2) to accept a bet.

CRAP OUT - in craps, to roll a two, three, or twelve on the first roll and lose.

CRAPS - 1) table game using two dice, each with spots representing the numbers one through six, 2) in the game of craps when a two, three, or twelve are rolled.

CRAPS DEALER - a casino employee who is in charge of the collection and pay off of wagers.

CRAP SHOOT OR CRAPS SHOOT - any venture where the result is unknown and, thus, a gamble.

CREDIT - 1) the custom in casinos where gamblers are allowed to bet without money so long as they agree to repay all losses they might incur, 2) in accounting, an entry on the right side of an account.

CREDIT MANAGER - casino employee who determines whether or not, and how much credit to allow a given player.

CREDIT SLIP - voucher or printed form that, when completed, accounts for the value of chips taken away from a table.

CRIMP - a cheating move where the corner of cards are bent so they can be identified later.

CROSSROADER - cheats who specialize in swindling the casino from the outside.

CROSS TRAINING - enables employees to learn the tasks associated with more than one job and, thus, fill in when necessary.

CROUPIER - a french word or term for gaming table employees.

CUCUMBER - an especially green or novice sucker.

CULL - cheating technique in cards where certain cards are sorted out of the deck for later use.

CULTURE - a group of people sharing a distinctive heritage or background, such as "corporate culture."

CUP - container in which dice are shaken, often made from leather.

CURATOR - in baccarat, the player whose turn it is to deal.

CURRENCY - coins and paper money.

CURRENT ASSETS - a financial term for organizational resources that can be converted to cash relatively easily.

CURRENT RATIO - a financial liquidity concept that compares current assets to current liabilities.

CUSHION- reserve bankroll.

CUSTOMER SERVICE - a management term referring to the policies set by the corporation and the extent to which the employees may go to satisfy the customers.

CUT - in card games, the splitting of the deck into two piles, then putting them back together in different order, and done to signify an unbiased shuffle.

CUT CARD - a divider, usually a solid piece of plastic put into the deck or the shoe to designate the time when the cards will be shuffled next.

CUT CHEQUES - when a dealer holds a stack of chips in one hand and uses the index finger to create a series of equal stacks. Also called thumb cut, drop cut.

CUT EDGE DICE - a method of cheating where the edges of each die are cut or shaved to larger and smaller angles with the result that the dice fall in the direction of the larger cut.

CUT IN - a cheating technique in craps where other dice are switched for those in play.

CUT INTO - matching a stack of a certain color chips with another stack of the same color.

CUTOUT WORK - a cheating technique in cards where a small part of the white section of the back design is extended with an acid or a knife that removes the ink, thus adding white area that was not there originally.

CUT TOKES - to divide the tips or gratuities between the dealers.

CUT UP JACKPOTS - to discuss openly about previous large wins and are usually exaggerated.

-D-

DATA - facts that have yet to be processed or organized for meaningful use.

DATABASE - in computers, a collection of retrievable information.

DAUB - a cheating move where cards are marked with coloring to facilitate later identification.

DAYS - expression used by casino employees to refer to the work shift that occurs during daylight, usually starting between 7 a.m. and noon.

DAY-TRIP MARKET - a market segment that can drive to the property and return home again the same day.

DEAD HEAD - 1) a patron who is out of money, 2) a non-player, 3) in Atlantic City, when a casino bus returns to the point of departure without the original passengers.

DEAD NUMBER DICE - a cheating technique in craps where dice are modified or loaded in such a way that one number comes up more often than statistically determined.

DEAD TABLE - table to which a dealer is assigned but has no players.

DEADWOOD PLAYERS - people who loiter in the casino but do not play, often due to lack of resources.

DEAL AROUND - when a dealer deliberately avoids giving cards to a player, often because the player is intoxicated.

DEALER - casino employee who conducts a table game who does not necessarily deal cards and is also called the croupier.

DEAL OUT - 1) the act by the dealer of getting the cards to the players, 2) to exclude a player from the game, deal out.

DEBIT or DB - in accounting, an entry on the left side of an account.

DEFERRED - understanding that the commission or vigorish will be paid later.

DELEGATION - in management, the process of assigning tasks and responsibility and granting authority to ensure that those tasks are accomplished.

DELIVERY - manner of getting the cards to the players.

DEMOGRAPHICS - objective and quantifiable population statistics that are easily identifiable and measurable such as age distribution, income, etc.

DE MOIVRE THEOREM - the rule that, during a series of trials within a Bernoulli system, the actual results will fluctuate from the mathematically determined result in direct proportion to the square root of the number of trials.

DENOMINATION - the value or rank of a card, chip, or cash.

DEPARTMENTATION - in management, the process of grouping activities or tasks into an organizational unit to accomplish some common purpose, such as the accounting department.

DEPRECIATION - an estimated measure of the value lost to an asset over a period of time, often set by the Internal Revenue Service.

DESTINATION MARKET - a market segment that stays over night, usually as a vacation.

DEUCE - 1) two dollars, 2) the two-spot on a die, 3) in cards, the two.

DICE - the plural of die and refers to the two objects that are played with in craps, each having six sides with spots representing the numbers of one to six.

DICE ARE OFF - dice that are not true, either from use or in an effort to cheat.

DICE BOAT - a container on the game table that retains the dice that are not being used.

DICE CHUTE - a plastic tube used to drop the dice in some games, designed to reduce the possibility of cheating over the use of a cup or throwing by hand.

DICE DEGENERATE - compulsive craps player who cannot control their need to gamble.

DICE PICKER - in craps, the casino employee whose task it is to retrieve dice that have fallen or been thrown off the table.

DIE - singular of dice and is a small cube with six sides and spots representing the numbers one to six.

DIFFERENTIATION STRATEGY - the approach a firm follows when it wants to be unique in its industry along dimensions widely valued by buyers.

DIME - wager of one thousand dollars.

DIRECT COSTS - expenses incurred by a firm that are in proportion to the output of a good or service.

DIRECT MARKETING - the process of attempting to reach the market directly through such media as mail or telephone. .

DIRTY MONEY - 1) chips from losing wagers that have not been returned to the bankroll, 2) money obtained through illegal means.

DISCARD - 1) playing card that is removed from the deck until the next shuffle, 2) used cards.

DISCARD HOLDER - receptacle, usually of metal or plastic, that is used to retain the discard.

DISCIPLINE - in business, actions taken by a manager to enforce the organization's standards and regulations.

DISCRETIONARY INCOME - a individual's or family's money that is left over after paying taxes and buying necessities.

DISPOSABLE INCOME - roughly, take-home pay, or that part of total income that is available for consumption or saving.

DIVERSIFICATION - a business strategy of adding products or services areas to the organization that are different from the current ones provided.

DOLLAR - a wager of one hundred dollars.

DOLLY - in roulette, the cylindrical object, usually of glass, that is used to designate the winning number.

DOMAIN - the market and the products or service areas in which the organization intends to operate.

DON'T COME - in craps, a bet placed after the come out roll. Depending on next roll either: 1) two or three wins; 2) a twelve is a standoff and; 3) seven or eleven loses.

DON'T PASS LINE - in craps, the zone where a player makes a don't pass bet.

DOORMAN - the casino employee who admits players to the gaming room, more common in Europe.

DOUBLE APRON - a cheating technique used by casino employees where their normally pocketless apron is modified to create a pocket where chips can be hidden.

DOUBLE DECK - in blackjack, when two hand held decks are used.

DOUBLE DOWN - in blackjack, an option that allows the player to double the value of their wager after looking at the first two cards.

DOUBLE DUKE - a cheating technique used by a dealer who deals his victim a very good hand but deals himself an even better one.

DOUBLE ENTRY BOOKKEEPING - a system for recording financial transactions in which every transaction creates entries that affect at least two accounts.

DOUBLE EXPOSURE - a variation of blackjack where both the dealer's cards are shown before bettors play their hands and may have rules changes to compensate for this advantage being given to the bettors.

DOUBLE ODDS - in craps and only in some casinos, when a player takes an odds bet at double the original stake.

DOUBLE UP - to enlarge a wager by an equal quantity.

DOUBLE ZERO - today, only American roulette wheels have two zeros, which is the thirty-eighth number on the wheel and green in color. The first casino roulette wheel had two zeros.

DOUBLING UP - to double the size of the preceding wager and serves as the basis for many betting strategies.

DRAG DOWN - to retrieve all or part of a wager just won, thus not letting it ride on the next bet.

DRAGGING - illegally removing chips from a wager after the game is in progress.

DRAW - 1) to take additional cards after the initial deal, 2) a form of poker.

DRILLER - a cheating technique at the slot machines where a hole is drilled in the machine so as to modify its play.

DROP - total amount of cash plus markers, during a given time frame. Can be at a table, on a shift, or in entire casino.

DROP BOX - box locked to the underside of a gaming table where the dealer deposits all currency , markers, and drop slips.

DROP BOX SLOT - an aperture in the table directly above the drop box which includes the cover or plunger that allows items to be placed in the drop box.

DROPPING - the act, during which the casino employee puts chips in the toke box.

DROP CUT - a method of holding a stack of chips in one hand, touching them to the table, then lifting them, leaving a small stack of the correct number of chips. Also called cut cheques, thumb cut.

DROWN - to lose heavily.

DRY - to lose all money, be broke, and can refer to a single individual or many.

DUE DILIGENCE - 1) in legal terms, the pre-trial activities to make every effort to obtain relevant facts to make the case, 2) a bundle of activities is a means to investigate or procure factual information garnered outside of the activities attendant on the formation, management and enforcement of a contract for casino credit.

DUKE - a big hand at a table.

DUMMY UP AND DEAL - old time Nevada phrase used by a boss to tell a dealer to stop talking and speed up the game.

DUMPING - to lose a great deal of money swiftly.

DUMPING OFF A GAME - a cheating technique where a dealer allows his accomplice to win money from the casino.

DUST HIM OFF - to flatter a player by suggesting they are very smart.

-E-

E.R. MAN - person who sits to the extreme right of the dealer, same as the anchor.

EARLY OUT - term used by dealers when they get the last break before the end of the shift and, thus, can go home early.

EARLY SURRENDER - in blackjack, the players option of relinquishing half the bet prior to the dealer determining if he has blackjack.

EARN - in casinos, the actual money the casinos can technically consider its take or revenue.

EARRING - a cheating technique used by dealers where they do not drop the paper money all the way into the drop box leaving one corner of the bill(s) exposed with the goal of retrieving it later. Also called hanger.

EASE OF ENTRY - occurs for business' when there are low capital requirements and no, or relatively low licensing provisions thus making it less difficult to begin a business.

EASY WAY - in craps, point made without paired numbers, e.g. making an eight with a five and a three rather than two fours, which is the hard way.

ECONOMETRIC MODELS - statistical methods of analyzing data and making predictions about the future.

ECONOMIC DEVELOPMENT - an economics term referring to the process by which less developed areas or regions increase their per capita output, whether by improving their stock of capital goods such as building a casino, improving worker's skills, or other means.

ECONOMIC IMPACT - an examination of the organization's effect on the external environments.

EDGE - the mathematical advantage, usually retained by the house.

EDGE WORK OR EDGE MARKINGS - a cheating technique in cards where they are marked with a slight bevel or belly drawn on certain point of each card between the design and the edge of the card.

EGO STRENGTHS - a personality characteristic that measures the potency of a persons convictions.

EIGHTY SIX - 1) used in casinos and restaurants, to eject, evict, or try to get rid of, 2) to close down a table, pit, or entire casino for the night.

ELECTRIC DICE - a cheating technique in craps where the dice are loaded with steel slugs and used over an electric magnet hidden in or under a counter or dice table.

ELEMENT OF RUIN - the probability that a player will lose their bank.

ELDEST HAND - the card player on the dealer's left.

E MAIL - an abbreviation for electronic mail, a technology that allows individuals to send and receive reports over computer networks.

EMPLOYEE - non-managerial workers of an organization who perform tasks and are responsible only for their own actions.

EMPLOYEE ASSISTANCE PROGRAMS or EAP - in companies, when counseling and other help is provided to workers having emotional, physical, or other personal problems.

EMPLOYEE BURNOUT - employees that do too much or have too much stress and become incapable of functioning effectively.

EMPOWERMENT - in business, increasing the decision making discretion of workers.

ENCODING - a psychological term referring to the process in which information from short term memory is entered into long term memory.

END OF DAY - an arbitrary stopping point for the business day, established so that the audit can be considered complete through that time frame and is often at an hour other than midnight.

ENFORCEMENT - the ability to compel a person to abide by the rules.

ENGLISH "AMERICAN" ROULETTE - a combination form of American Roulette begun with the British Gaming Act of 1968, where the double zero from the American type is eliminated, player differentiated chips are used, there is a single zero derived from the French version, when zero appears the share half concession is used.

EN PLEIN - in roulette, french term for a wager on a single number.

EN PRISON - french term used in roulette which permits the player to let his wager ride or surrender only half of it if a zero or double zero shows up.

ENTREPRENEURSHIP - a business term which refers to a process through which new business is created that involves uncertainty, risk, creative opportunism, and orientation toward growth.

ENTROPY - the tendency or an organization to deteriorate.

EUROPEAN PLAN - in hotels, a billing arrangement under which meals are priced separately from rooms.

ENVIRONMENTAL SCANNING - in management, a method o
identifying emerging environmental opportunities and threats
that may influence the organization's performance.

EQUAL EMPLOYMENT OPPORTUNITY or EEO - in
management, employment related decision must not be made
based on factors such as race, color, religion, sex, national
origin, or handicapped status.

**EQUAL EMPLOYMENT OPPORTUNITY COMMISSION
or EEOC** - federal government agency created to administer
the provisions of the Civil Rights Acts of 1964, which contains
laws regulating the staffing or organizations.

EQUITABLE - a fair game.

EQUITY CAPITAL - funds supplied by the owner(s) of a
business in return for the opportunity to share in the risks and
rewards of the business.

EVEN CHANCES or EVEN MONEY - odds of one to one.

EVENING SHIFT - time frame for working that usually covers
from 3 p.m. to 11 p.m.

EVEN UP - a wager made on even odds.

EXACT COUNT - equal to the running count divided by the
conversion factor to indicate what the count would be if the
game were being dealt from a single deck. Thus, if the running
count is 12, and three decks remain to be played, the exact
count is twelve dived by three thus equalling four, indicating to
the player that there is a relative surplus of two tens per fifty-
two cards left to be played.

EXPECTANCY THEORY - in management, a theory of
motivation based on probability and the relationships between
efforts, performance, and rewards.

EXPECTED VALUE - the money the player should win or lose
given average luck or in accordance with the statistical
advantage of the casino. Thus, the expected value equals the
player's advantage in percent multiplied by the total action.

XTERNAL AUDIT - review of a firm's finances accomplished by a public accounting firm.

EXTERNAL ENVIRONMENTAL FORCES - factors outside the organization's control, including suppliers, customers, government, and unions, that may affect performance and decision making.

EXTERNALITIES - an activity that affects others, for better or worse, without those others paying or being paid for the activity, as in crime being suggested as a negative externality of casino gaming.

EXTRINSIC REWARDS - management term referring to rewards such as pay, promotion, praise and benefits that an employee receives from others.

EYE or EYE IN THE SKY - surveillance equipment suspended from the ceiling and tied into a central observation point.

-F-

FACE CARDS - jack, queen, or king.

FACE DOWN - method of delivering cards so that only the player sees them.

FAD - a very short-lived fashion or trend.

FADE - to cover all or part of the shooter's center bet.

FADE COVER - in craps or chemin de fer, a bet against the bank.

FADING GAME - open craps.

FAITES VOS JEUX - French for "Place your bets" and signals the start of betting at the roulette table.

FAIR GAME - a game in which the payoffs are equal to the mathematical chances of winning. Casino games are not fair since the casino's payoffs are somewhat less than the mathematical probability of each result, and this small advantage will prove decisive over a long series of trials.

FALSE CARDING - in Draw Poker, bluffing by taking fewer cards than is necessary to improve one's hand so that a position of strength is implied.

FAN TAN - simple oriental game played with beans or buttons where the outcome is decided by a dealer dividing a pile of buttons with a stick, separating four at a time until four, then three, then one is left. Found in some Nevada casinos.

FAVORITES - numbers or chances coming up frequently during certain times of a particular game.

FAN - to lay the deck of cards out on the table for observation and verification.

FARO - card game using a bank, where cards selected from the deck win sequentially or alternately, for the bank and the players.

FAT - person who has a large quantity of money, is loaded.

FAX - abbreviation for electronic facsimile.

F&B - short for food and beverage.

FEVER - 1) gambling habit, 2) in craps, the number five.

FIELD - in craps, a wager good only for the next roll.

FILL - bringing additional checks from the cage to the table to replenish the dealer's bankroll.

FILL SLIP - voucher that goes along with the fill, is verified, and signed with one copy deposited in the drop box and one copy given to the floorperson by the dealer.

FIN - five dollar bill.

FINALS - in roulette, the right most digits of the numbers on the wheel.

FINGER - to identify a cheat.

FIRM - 1) to hold or maintain one's wager, 2) business unit.

FIRST BASE - in blackjack, the first seat or position, immediately to the dealer's left and the player who receives the first card dealt.

FIRST BASING - a cheating technique in blackjack where the player in the first seat reads the dealer's hole card when it is picked up to see if he has a natural.

FIX - to influence the outcome of a sports event or game in order to win a wager.

FIXED COST - financial liabilities that remain static or that do not vary with changes in business volume.

FLAG - a die that has been modified so that it is not true.

FLAGGED - in craps, to be passed by as the next shooter.

FLASH - to display a card, usually the dealer's hole card.

FLASHING - a cheating technique in blackjack where the dealer exposes the top card of the deck to an accomplice to help him win.

FLASH WORK - a cheating technique in cards where the entire back of each card except for one small portion is shaded lightly.

FLAT BET - to bet the same amount on each hand played.

FLAT ORGANIZATION - internal structure of a business where a large number of subordinates report to one supervisor, and characteristic of new or small business'.

FLEA - 1) a leech of a patron who tries to ride on the laurels of an ardent gambler or who loiters in the casino attempting to get comps or other privileges, 2) derogatory term used by casino employees for a small bettor.

FLOAT - in a table game, the tray.

FLOAT COVER - the lid of the chip tray which locks.

FLOATER - in roulette, when the ball hangs up under the lip and will not drop.

FLOATS - dice that are not true because they have been hollowed out and, thus are so light they seem to float.

FLOOR PLAN - the most common and informative type of blueprint, sometimes referred to as a plan view, which takes a straight down or birds eye perspective, often showing things like the position of gaming tables, cashiers, dining tables, etc.

FLOPPING THE DECK - a cheating technique in blackjack where the dealer secretly turns the deck over so the used, face up cards on the bottom are dealt again.

FLOORMAN or FLOOR PERSON - supervisor of the gaming tables who is responsible for keeping the racks full, attends to any problems at the tables, supervises the dealers, and watches for irregularities.

FLUSH - 1) gambler who is winning or has a lot of money, 2) in poker, a hand containing any five cards of one suit.

FOLD, FOLDING - throwing in a hand of cards or dropping out.

FOREIGN CHECKS - chips from another casino.

FOLIO or GUEST FOLIO - in hotels, a collection of guest charges that are recorded either manually or by computer.

FORMAL COMMUNICATIONS CHANNELS - in an organization, those communication flows that follow the formal organizational relationships depicted by an organization chart.

FOUR OF A KIND - in poker, all four cards are the same rank.

FRANCHISING - a contractual arrangement between a franchisor (who owns the name and style of operation) and a franchisee, that allows the franchisee to conduct business under an established name and according to a given pattern of business in return for a fee. Widely used in hotels and chain restaurants.

FREEZE OUT - to force a gambler out of a game.

FRENCH WHEEL - European roulette wheel which contains only one zero located between black twenty six and red thirty two.

FRETS - in roulette, the dividers that create the pockets on the wheel.

FRONT DESK - in lodging, the focal point of activity within the front office, usually located in the lobby and where the guest checks in, is assigned a room, and checks out.

FRONT LINE - in craps, the pass line.

FRONT LOADER - in blackjack, a careless dealer who uncovers his hole card while dealing.

FRONT MAN - a person who does not have a criminal record who poses as the owner of a casino when he really is not, and is done in an effort to circumvent the law.

FRONT MONEY - funds put forth by a player to establish credit in a casino.

FRONT OF THE HOUSE - the functional areas of the casino, hotel, or restaurant in which employees have extensive guest contact such as the casino floor, front desk, or dining room.

FRUIT MACHINE - Term used by the English for a slot machine, because the earliest slot reels used fruit as symbols.

FULL HOUSE - in poker, a hand with three of a kind plus a pair.

FULL MOON - term used by dealers to refer to the time of the month when, they think, all the strange people or turkeys come to their table.

FULL TABLE - a crowded craps table.

FUNCTIONAL AUTHORITY - in management, the authority to make decisions and prescribe policies, procedures, and other matters for a specialized area of operations such as accounting, finance, etc.

-G-

G or GAFF or GIMMICK - any secret cheating device.

GALLOPING DOMINOES - pair of dice.

GAMBLER'S FALLACY - the erroneous belief that because an event has not occurred recently in a series of independent trials, it becomes more likely to occur in the future.

GAMBLER'S RUIN - the risk that a gambler will run out of money or lose their entire bankroll.

GAMBLING - to make a prediction of an uncertain outcome and then back the decision with money.

GAMES - casino gaming activities that use dealers, and does not include slot machines.

GAMING BOARD or COMMISSION - in some jurisdictions, the name of the government appointed authority that regulates casino gaming.

GATE - in craps, when an official or employee of the casino stops the dice before they have finished rolling because they fear fowl play.

GEORGE - 1) a player who plays very well, 2) player who gives the dealer cash, 3) player who makes bets on behalf of the dealer.

GET BEHIND THE STICK - in craps, when a stickman or dealer goes to work or opens the game.

G.I. MARBLES - dice.

GIMMICK - something used to fix or alter a game.

GIVE HIM THE BUM'S RUSH - to eject a player without dignity.

GIVE THE BUSINESS - to cheat someone.

GLASS HOUSE - a management term referring to the situation where all decisions and actions are viewed by any and everyone.

GLIM - a cheating technique which employs a small hidden mirror that allows the cheat to see the faces of the cards as they are dealt.

GM - short for general manager.

G-NOTE - one thousand dollar bill.

GO - term used by dealers when talking about the amount of tips made, as in "What did you go yesterday?"

GOOD MAN - 1) a player with much money, 2) someone who is an adept cheater.

GOOD THING - a sound wager.

GOOSE - in keno, the tube where balls collect after being forced there by an air stream.

GO OVER - in blackjack, when anyone exceeds twenty-one. Also called break or bust.

41

GO SOUTH WITH - to secretly palm cards, dice, money, or anything else and take it out of action.

GRAND - one thousand dollars.

GRAPEVINE - in an organization, the informal, lateral communications through which a few individuals relate information to others.

GRAVEYARD SHIFT - the last work shift, usually lasting until early morning.

GRAVITY MODEL - a computer site-selection method based on the premise that people frequent business' that are closer and more attractive than competitors'.

GREEK DEAL - a cheating technique where the second card from the bottom of the deck is dealt while pretending to deal off the top.

GREEK SHOT - in craps, a controlled throw of the dice.

GREEN - 1) cash, 2) twenty- five dollar chips that are green in color.

GREEN HORN - an inexperienced gambler.

GREEN NUMBERS - in roulette, the zero and double zero.

GRIEF - bad luck or difficulty.

GRIEVANCE PROCEDURE - a formal channel of communication, often found in companies with unions, used to resolve job related complaints.

GRIFTER - a dishonest gambler.

GRIND HOUSES OR JOINT - casinos catering to low-end players (low rollers) but requiring high volume of play.

GROSS REVENUES - in accounting, total incoming sales.

GROUP NORMS - unwritten rules of conduct established to maintain consistent and desired behavior within the group, often found in business.

-H-

HAND - 1) in a card game like blackjack, the player's cards, 2) in craps, the total length of time and number of rolls of one shooter from the come out roll.

HANDICAPPER - track official who assigns weights to certain horses in a race.

HANDICAP ROOM - in lodging, a guestroom with special features designed to meet the needs of handicapped guests.

HANDLE - total amount of money that changes hands over and over through a series of bets before it is actually won or lost.

HAND MUCKER - a cheating move in cards, where the perpetrator palms or switches the cards he has been dealt.

HAND OFF - a cheating technique where the dealer secretly transfers chips to an associate who is posing as a player.

HANDLE SLAMMING - a cheating technique at the slot machines where the cheat tries to control the reel combination that comes up by first pulling the handle, then slamming it back upward.

HANGER - a cheating technique where the dealer does not drop paper money all the way into the box leaving a corner exposed with the expectation of retrieving it later. Also called earring.

HARD COUNT - counting of hard money (coins).

HARD HAND or HARD TOTAL - in blackjack, a hand that does not include an ace, or in which an ace can only be valued as one if the total of the hand is not to exceed twenty-one.

HARD OPENING - a term that refers to the complete operation being totally functional at the hour of inauguration of the property.

HARD WAY - in craps, the numbers four, six, eight, and ten made by having the dice come up as a pair such as two fives to make ten rather than a six and a four.

HAS A SIGN ON HIS BACK - gambler who is known on sight by the casinos and is regarded as a cheater.

HAY - money or chips.

HEAD - 1) in roulette, the part of the wheel that spins and fits into the bowl, 2) the restroom.

HEAD COUNT - number of people.

HEAD ON - when a player is alone at the table and is playing against the dealer.

HEART - courage, fortitude, guts.

HEAT - 1) in blackjack, statements by casino employees that suggest to a player that they are suspected of card counting, 2) heavy surveillance which tends to reduce cheating, 3) close scrutiny, pressure, or criticism of the dealer by bosses.

HEAVY HAND - a hand of cards that, unbeknown to others, has more cards than it is supposed to.

HEEL - 1) a stingy gambler, 2) a jerk, 3) to separate a wager made with more than one color of chip, 4) to place one cheque of a marker on top of another cheque angled in the direction of the player.

HIERARCHY - in management, the division of authority among levels of management.

HIERARCHY OF EFFECT MODEL - the sequence of steps a consumer goes through, in reacting to promotion, that leads them from awareness to knowledge to liking to preference to conviction to purchase.

HIGH/LOW - in craps, a split bet on two and twelve.

HIGH ROLLER OR HIGH STAKES GAMBLERS- anyone able and willing to spend $5,000 or more in a weekend of gambling. There are an estimated 35,000 high rollers in the world.

HIT - in blackjack, to request another card from the dealer.

HIT AND RUN - to win quickly and then leave the game.

HIT IT - to make the desired point or number.

HIT THE BOARDS - 1) to leave or depart, 2) in craps, when the stick man asks the shooter to be sure to throw the dice against the rail.

HOLD - proportion of player outlays retained by the house after redeeming chips and slot machine tokes.

HOLD OUT - a cheating technique where cards are kept out of play with the plan of later switching them for cards that have been dealt.

HOLD PERCENTAGE - the amount of money won by the casino expressed as a percentage of the amount of money or credit exchanged for gaming chips (the drop).

HOLE CARD - 1) a card dealt face down or concealed in blackjack or poker, 2) in blackjack, the dealer's bottom card usually dealt face down.

HOLE CARD PLAY - any of a number of cheating techniques in blackjack where the cheat tries to catch a glimpse of the dealer's hole card.

HOOK - a half point in a bet on a sporting event that eliminates a tie, as in "I've got the Raiders by half a point."

HOOKED - to lose money.

HOP - a cheating technique where cards are brought back to their original order after being cut by another player.

HORIZON - in lodging, the future time frame for which a reservation is accepted.

HOSPITALITY OPERATIONS - the management of the activities involved in producing the goods or services of an organization involved in sheltering, feeding, transporting, and entertaining people.

HOT - 1) in craps, when dice make more passes than misses, 2) in a card game, when the deck or shoe is favorable to the player.

HOUSE - casino, casino employees, casino's funds or bank.

HOUSE ADVANTAGE or PERCENTAGE - mathematical winning edge that the casino gives itself by manipulating the rules of the games to ensure profitability.

HOUSE DEALER - dealer who is winning.

HOUSE LIMIT - a credit limit established by the casino or hotel.

HOUSE NUMBERS - in roulette, the zero and double zero which, when they come up, allows a profit for the casino in all even money bets.

HOST - casino employee whose job is to ensure valued or rated players are kept satisfied with the casino and its services. They also handle some marketing, promotions, invitations to special events, etc.

HUB - 1) in computers, a central location for processing before the information is dispersed, 2) in transportation, a central terminal from which all transportation leaves and returns.

HUMAN CAPITAL - the stock of technical skill and knowledge embodied in a region's work force, resulting from formal education and on-the-job training.

HUMAN RESOURCES - the department that focuses on the people in the organization.

HUMAN RESOURCES INFORMATION SYSTEM or HRIS - an integrated computerized system designed to provide information to be used in making personnel decisions.

HUNCH PLAYERS - a gambler who bets impulsively with little knowledge of the game.

HUSTLING - actions that induce a gift or a tip.

HYPSTER - a cheater who specializes in shortchanging cashiers.

-I-

ICE - protection money.

ICEMAN - bagman, person who collects money.

IMAGE - refers to how a business is viewed, either positively or negatively, by consumers.

IMPAIR - in roulette, wagering that the winning number will be odd.

IN - quantity of money that a player has traded for chips at the table. Also called a buy-in.

IN BALANCE - an accounting term used to describe the state when the totals of debit amounts and credit amounts are equal.

INCENTIVES - in management, rewards designed to encourage and reimburse employees for efforts beyond normal performance expectations.

INCOME - the flow of wages, interest, dividends, and other receipts accruing to an individual, firm, or region.

INCOME STATEMENT - financial statement that encapsulates the performance of an organization for a specified period of time.

INDEX - the numbers in the upper left and lower right of a player card that indicate its value.

INDIAN DICE - a traditional Native American bar game using 5 dice and allowed under Class I gaming. Each player gets three throws. The object is to build the best possible poker hand. Other rules include a one as wild and there are no straights.

INDIAN GAMING - a term referring to the betting on uncertain outcomes on Native American reservations.

INDIAN GAMING REGULATORY ACT or IGRA - a 1988 federal regulation which established rules and three levels for Native American gambling. (see Class I, Class II and Class III).

INDICATOR - on the big six wheel, the clapper that indicates the winning space.

INDUSTRY - group of firms or business' producing similar goods or services.

INNOVATION - in business, the creation or acquisition of new technology.

INNOVATOR - 1) in management, a person who is creative and approaches problems from a new perspective, 2) in marketing, a person who tries new products first.

IN PRISON - in European roulette, when all bets are held on even money until the next spin caused when the ball lands on zero.

INPUTS - raw data that are entered in the information system.

INSIDE - the casino's position in the games.

INSIDE MAN - casino employee who handles the books or finances.

INSIDE STRAIGHT - in poker, a sequence of cards that needs an internal or middle card to complete the sequence.

INSURANCE - in blackjack, a wager that the dealer has a ten card face down when an ace is showing and which pays two to one.

INSURANCE LINE - in blackjack, the place on the table where the insurance bet is placed.

INTERDEPENDENCY - when changes in one part of the organization affect all other parts of the organization.

INTERMODAL TRANSPORTATION - the use of a combination of transportation modes to take advantage of the benefits of each mode during its portion of the transportation task as in using planes then busses to transport people to a casino.

INTERNAL AUDIT - financial review preformed by company personnel.

INTERNAL ENVIRONMENT - tangible and intangible factors that exist with the organization and are under its control.

INTERNAL ORGANIZATIONAL FORCES - factors inside the organization including personnel, organization structure, policies, resources, and relationships that may affect managerial decision making.

IN THE CHIPS - to have a lot of money.

IN THE CLEAR - free of debt.

IN THE RED - 1) in debt, 2) losing, 3) out of money.

INTRINSIC REWARDS - rewards that originate with the person due to satisfaction with the work itself, achievements, and self -esteem.

-J-

JACKPOT - largest payout a slot machine makes.

JETON - French chip or token.

JIMBRONI - a slow thinking dealer.

JIT - five cents.

JOB DESCRIPTION - an outline of the basic tasks, duties, and responsibilities of a particular work assignment.

JOB SPECIFICATION - the qualifications such as knowledge, skills, and abilities required of a person to perform a work assignment satisfactorily.

JOG - a cheating technique where a card protrudes slightly from the deck to act as a marker and used during illegal shuffles and cuts.

JOHNSON ACT - federal legislation passed in the 1950's that abolished any use of slot machines.

JOINT - a casino.

JOINT BANK - situation where two players combine their resources and play jointly off the total sum, sharing in the win or loss.

JOINT VENTURE - a partnership between an organization and host firm, or two firms, to finance and manage a cooperatively owned enterprise, often found in Native American Casinos.

JUG - jail.

JUICE - 1) power, influence, knowing the right people, 2) in baccarat the vigorish, 3) electricity.

JUICE JOINT - a cheating technique where the roulette wheel or dice game is electronically controlled.

JUNKET - a form of comp where a group of people who are known and rated gamblers are brought to the casino on an all inclusive trip paid for by the casino and are expected to participate in a given level of casino action.

-K-

KENO - a lottery type of casino game where players win by picking certain of up to twenty numbers which are subsequently drawn from among eighty numbers and is often played off the casino floor. One number pays two to one on three to one odds, thus giving the casino a twenty five percent edge, with the more number the players chooses commensurately increasing the odds.

KIBITZER - spectator who often makes unsolicited and unwanted comments to the players.

KING KONG - in dealer's jargon, a player who bets a lot for the dealer.

KITTY - a pool of money, which goes either in its entirety, or in part, to the winner of a hand or round of wagering.

KNOCK OUT - a cheating term in a casino referring to when a dealer takes all the money from a player as in " I cleaned out the guy from New York."

-L-

LABOR FORCE or SUPPLY - the availability of trained and willing workers in a region so as to fill organizational positions.

LACE - in baccarat, a technique for mixing the cards after the shuffle.

LADDER MAN - casino employee who sits on a high stool or platform to oversee and supervise the game.

LAMMERS - 1) small discs used to show the value of a chip or check, 2) signify the use of credit, 3) someone who is running away, usually from the law.

LAN - in computers, a local area network of computers.

LAND BASED CASINO - a casino that is totally constructed and physically supported on the land, rather than on water.

LATE BET - in roulette, placing a winning wager after the call has been made for no more bets.

LAW OF DEMAND - theory that consumers usually purchase more units at low prices than at high prices.

LAY AND PAY - approach of turning over a players cards or taking wagers followed by gathering up all the used cards at once as in "Most of the joints are lay and pay."

LAY BET - in craps, a wager that seven will roll before the number wagered on. A house commission is charged on the true dice odds amount that could be won.

LAY DOWN - a bet or wager.

LAYOUT - 1) the diagram on a gaming table, usually in green, sometimes in red, rarely in blue and imprinted in white, 2) internal design .

LEADERSHIP - in management, an activity that consists of influencing other people's behavior, individual and as a group, toward the achievement of desired objectives.

LEAK - to fail to completely hide a cheating move such as allowing a palmed card to show between the cheat's fingers.

LE GRAND - in baccarat, when two cards total nine.

LET IT RIDE - to replay a winning bet including the original bet and the winnings.

LEVELS - any honest gaming equipment, particularly dice.

LEVERAGE - financial concept that compares the proportion of funds provided internally to those proved by external creditors.

LIABILITIES - financial term that refers to debts owed by a firm.

LIFE CYCLE - the useful life of a product in a given market which includes the stages of introduction, growth, maturity, and decline.

LIFE STYLES - the ways in which individual consumers and families or households live and spend time and money.

LIGHT - 1) any device that allows the cheat to observe the cards as he deals them, same as a glim, 2) insufficient amount, 3) weak.

LIGHT BET - a wager that is below the table minimum.

LIGHT WORK - altered cards marked with very fine lines.

LIMIT - maximum or minimum bet allowed.

LINE - amount of credit a player has with the casino.

LINEAR PROGRAMMING - mathematical aid for decision makers who wish to maximize some desired objective or minimize some undesired result, subject to limitations.

LINE BUS - in casinos, the bus program where the carriers charge a fare and organize it.

LINE WORK - on altered cards, additional small spots, curlicues, or lines added to the back design of the cards so that they can be read by the cheat.

LIQUIDITY RATIOS - financial ratios that indicate the capability of an organization to pay its debts.

LOAD - in craps, a method of cheating where weight is placed inside the dice to alter the characteristics.

LOADER - careless dealer who shows the hole card while dealing.

LOCKED UP - when a dealer has to stay working a game for longer than normal, without a break.

LOCK UP - to safely store money in the toke box or rack.

LOCUS OF CONTROL - an organizational theory term that refers to a personality attribute that measures the degree to which people believe they are masters of their own fate.

LONG BET - a wager that exceeds the table limit.

LONG GREEN - cash, paper money.

LOOKING FOR ACTION - a gambler looking for a game.

LOOKOUT - a casino employee who acts as an observer of the floor or games to ensure smooth operations, through surveillance.

LOOSE - 1) in slot machines, a unit with a high pay back rate, 2) a person with low morals or one who is promiscuous.

LOTTERY - in gaming, a randomized drawing from a pool, usually of sold tickets.

LOW ROLLER - typical tourist making one and two dollar bets, also known as grinds, suckers, or tinhorns.

LUCK - 1) the inexplicable, 2) anything not due to skill, statistics, or science.

LUGGER - an individual who delivers gamblers to a game.

LUMINOUS READERS - a cheating technique in cards where a substance in placed on the backs of the cards that can only be seen through tinted glasses.

-M-

MACHIAVELLIANISM - a measure of the degree to which people are pragmatic, maintain emotional distance, and believe that ends justify means.

MACHINE, HOLDOUT MACHINE - a mechanical device worn on the cheaters chest that allows them to retain certain cards and keep them out of play until later.

MAGNET - in cheating, a person who places a magnet on the side of the older slot machines to get the inside wheels to line up and then pulls the magnet off.

MALLARD - one hundred dollar bill.

MANAGEMENT - the effective and efficient integration and coordination or resources in order to achieve desired objectives.

MANAGEMENT CONTRACT - an agreement between the owner/developer of a facility and a professional management company where the owner/developer usually retains the financial and legal responsibility for the facility while the management company receives an agreed upon fee and/or percentage for operating the facility.

MANAGEMENT FUNCTIONS - the major activities of management including planning, organizing, directing, and controlling.

MANAGEMENT INFORMATION SYSTEM or MIS - an organized method of providing past, present, and projected information relating to internal and external operations to assist in decision making.

MANAGER - person in an organization who undertakes management in including planning, organizing, directing, and controlling and, thus, coordinates activities in order to guide the organization towards its desired goals.

MAN UPSTAIRS - 1) casino employee's term for top management, 2) the casino employees who work in surveillance monitoring the cameras of the eye in the sky.

MARK - the target of a con man.

MARKER - an I.O.U. or credit extended to a player.

MARKER CARD - a card positioned in the deck or shoe to signify the end of play.

MARKER DOWN - a communicative phrase to the floorperson indicating that the marker has been repaid.

MARKETING MIX - the combination of variables over which marketers have control which include price, product, place, and promotion.

MARKET NICHE - usually a small and specialized portion of a market, sometimes called a segment.

MARKET SEGMENT - a specific group of consumers.

MARKET SHARE - fraction of an industry's output accounted for by an individual firm or group of firms.

MARK OFF - the process by which the dealer separates stacks of chips in the rack into the proper size, so that a floorperson can quickly and accurately count them from a distance.

MARTINGALE - in roulette, a doubling up system of wagering.

MASON - a stingy player.

MAXIMUM - the largest bets allowed per chance and per player, as set by the casino.

MEAN - 1) nasty person, 2) in statistics, the same as average.

MECHANIC - a dealer who is very good at cheating and manipulating the cards.

MECHANICAL GAMES - games that demand little or no skill such as slot machines or pull tabs.

MECHANISTIC ORGANIZATION - an organization that tends to be inflexible and, thus, resistant to change.

MEDIAN - in mathematics, the figure in the exact middle of a series of numbers ordered or ranked from lowest to highest.

MEGA-RESORTS - a self contained, destination property that includes, at a minimum, hotel, restaurants, swimming pools, tennis courts, and other amenities.

MEMPHIS DOMINOES - dice.

MENTOR - a person who sponsors, supports, or guides another employee who is lower in the organization.

MEXICAN STANDOFF - a wagering session that ends in either incidental winnings or losses.

MICHIGAN BANKROLL - wads of money where a large denomination bill is wrapped around a core of one dollar bills in an effort to make the player appear to have more money.

MINI BACCARAT - a baccarat game played on a smaller, blackjack style table, with one dealer who distributes all the cards, rather than passing the shoe from player to player and usually has lower minimum wagers than baccarat.

MINIMUM - the lowest wager allowed to be placed at a table.

MISSION - the stated and basic written objective of the organization which serves to guide it and is conveyed to others through the mission statement.

MISSOUT - in craps, failure to make the point.

MIXED STACK - a pile of chips that contains several denominations or colors.

MODE OF TRANSPORTATION - transportation option that is chosen such as airplane, bus, boat, car, etc.

MONEY, CLEAN - the casino's money.

MONEY, DIRTY - lost wagers brought to the chip tray.

MONEY WHEEL - the big six wheel.

MONITOR - part of the surveillance system where the output from the eye in the sky is displayed.

MONKEY - 1) face card, 2) a sucker.

MONOPOLISTIC COMPETITION - in economics, a term referring to a market structure in which there is a large number of sellers who are supplying goods that are close, but not perfect, substitutes.

MORNING LINE - in horse and dog racing, the handicapper's or pricemaker's morning guess as to the probable odds that are to run in the afternoon races.

MOTIVATION - the sum of the energizing forces, both internal and external to a person, that account, in part, for certain behaviors.

MOUTHPIECE - a lawyer.

MOVE - 1) sleight of hand cheating technique, 2) to cheat using slight of hand.

MUCK - a cheating technique where one or all of the cards one has been dealt in a game are switched for previously palmed cards.

MUCKER - 1) a cheater who uses palming and switching techniques, 2) in roulette, the second dealer who facilitates payoffs and in cleaning up checks.

MUG PUNTER - a gambler who does not even have a rudimentary knowledge of the odds and probabilities in a game which they are playing.

MULTIDIMENSIONAL SCALING - a statistical technique that allows attitudinal data to be collected for several attributes in a manner that yields a single overall rating.

MULTIPLE ACTION BLACKJACK - version of blackjack which allows wagerers to play up to three hands at one time and to make three bets, all from the same deck.

MULTIPLIER - in regional economics, a tern used to denote the change in an induced variable (GNP, money supply, tourism spending) per unit change in an external variable (government spending, tax rates, building a casino).

-N-

NAIL - to catch someone cheating.

NAIL WORK - a cheating technique where the person presses a thumb or fingernail into the edge of a card to leave a telltale identification that can be seen across the table and felt when the cheat is dealing.

NATIONAL INDIAN GAMING ASSOCIATION or NIGA - represents the Native American gaming tribes in Washington, D.C.

NATIVE AMERICAN - a term referring to people who settled in the U.S. before the Europeans arrived.

NATURAL - 1) in blackjack, a two card count of twenty-one,
2) in craps, a seven or eleven on the come-out roll,
3) in baccarat, a two card count of eight or nine.

NECKTYING - A cheating technique where the dealer tilts the front end of the deck upward to hide a second deal.

NEEDS - a person's physical and psychological desires.

NEGATIVE SWING - a period during which a loss is shown, even with a mathematical advantage.

NEGOTIATION - the process in which two or more parties want to exchange goods or services and attempt to agree upon a suitable exchange rate.

NEIGHBORS - in roulette, numbers that are in proximity on the wheel.

NEPOTISM - the practice of hiring one's own relatives to work in the same organization.

NET CASH RECEIPTS - the amount of cash and checks in the register drawer, minus the amount of the initial cash bank.

NET INVESTMENT - the gross investment minus depreciation of capital goods.

NET LOSS - the negative result of deducting gross expenses, including taxes, from gross revenues.

NET PROFIT - the gross profit minus operating expenses.

NETWORKING - 1) linking computers to communicate with each other, 2) people meeting others in their profession in order to help each other.

NET WORTH - total assets minus total liabilities.

NEW PRODUCT DEVELOPMENT PROCESS - process used to evaluate, develop, and launch new products.

NICHE - a unique position that separates a product or organization from its competitors. For example, adding an amusement park to the hotel when no other competitors have one will create a niche for the hotel.

NICKEL - five dollar chips.

NIGHT AUDIT - in accounting, the daily review of guest accounts against revenue center transaction information.

NIGHT AUDITOR - in hotels, the employee who checks the accuracy of front office accounting records and compiles a daily summary of hotel financial data.

NIGHT SHIFT - work shift generally from eleven p.m. to seven a.m.

NO BRAINER - a slang term for a decision that is so easy that a person could make it correctly without thinking.

NO DICE - a craps term referring to a disallowed roll of the dice, frequently because they failed to hit a wall or did not land straight.

NOIR - a roulette term referring to a bet for the winning number to be black.

NOISE - in the communication process, any disturbances that interfere with transmission of a message.

NOMINAL SCALE - in creating a research design, the measurement instrument codes the responses as numbers solely for the purpose of identification. For example, assigning "male" an 11 and "female" 21 just to distinguish the gender difference.

NON-AFFILIATE RESERVATION NETWORK - central reservation system which connects independent properties.

NON-AUTOMATED - a system of front office record keeping that exclusively uses handwritten forms.

NON-GUARANTEED RESERVATION - when the hotel agrees to hold a room until a stated time but no payment is received if the guest does not show up.

NON-GUEST ACCOUNT - an account created to track the financial transactions of organizations who use the facilities of the hotel.

NON-GUEST FOLIO - a statement of transactions for a non-guest business or agency that has hotel charge purchase privileges.

NON-MONETARY COMPENSATION - recompense other than money that includes items like trips, awards, or recognition.

NON-PRICE COMPETITION - a strategy where price is fixed for everyone and therefore other factors must be used like advertising or product differentiation, as a basis for competition.

NONVERBAL COMMUNICATION - an aspect of communication that refers to meanings that are transmitted without words. For example, when poker players watch their opponents' faces for positive or negative reactions to the cards.

NO-POST STATUS - guest who is not allowed to charge purchases to the room.

NORMAL DISTRIBUTION - a statistical term that refers to the symmetrical, bell-shaped curve that large numbers of data points form around the expected or average outcome. For example, if the odds are equal, a gambler would expect that half the time he would win and half the time he would lose. If these points were plotted on a graph, they would form a normal distribution around the mid-point.

NORMATIVE INFLUENCE - in organizational behavior, a natural process of groups of people is that they set and enforce their ideas of conduct. For example, if a group of people go to the casino together, they will influence each other to stay longer and bet more.

NORMATIVE SOCIAL INFLUENCE - when a person allows behavior to be altered in order to meet the expectations of a person or group. For example, Sam doesn't want to go to the casino but his wife does. So he goes to keep peace in the family.

NORMS - informal rules of conduct. For example, in America, tips are expected, while in Japan, tipping is considered an insult. This is an unwritten social expectation.

NOSER - short for a drawer or bank that balanced at the end of the shift.

NO-SHOW - a person who makes a reservation but does not cancel and does not show up.

NUMBER TWO MAN - a cheating move where the dealer deals the second card from the top.

NUT - 1) overhead expenses, 2) the amount a casino must make to break even.

-O-

OBJECTIVE - a strategic planning term that refers to the measurable goal which an organization plans to reach in a specific time frame. For example, a company plans a five percent growth rate for the company by next January first.

OBSERVATIONAL LEARNING - when people learn by watching others. For example, people watch the table play in order to learn the game before sitting down to play.

OCCUPANCY DATA - in casinos, actual count of individual machine usage.

OCCUPANCY PERCENTAGE - a statistical term that shows that ratio of the "proportion of rooms sold" to "rooms available for sale" during a specific period of time, expressed as a percentage.

OCCUPANCY REPORT - front office statement containing which rooms were sold and inhabited.

OCCUPIED - the front office term for a room where a guest is currently registered.

OCTANT - in roulette, a term referring to a group of any five numbers which are physically adjacent around the wheel.

ODDS - ratio or probability that one event will happen over another.

OFF - in craps, a term that a bet is "off" or not in action for a specific roll of the dice.

OFFICE - any kind of secret sign given between cheats.

OFF-NUMBER BET - in craps, a bet that the shooter will or won't throw a specified number other than his point before throwing a seven.

OFF NUMBERS - in craps, the box numbers including four, five, six, eight, nine, and ten.

OFF-THE-TOP - in card games, the beginning of the deck or shoe immediately after the shuffle.

OFF-THE-STREET - getting a job without knowing anyone at the casino. For example, Joe came in "off the street".

OFF TRACK BETTING or OTB - betting that takes place other than at the actual race track.

OLIGOPOLY - in economics, a term referring to the competitive environment where a few large corporations control the market.

ON-CHANGE - a front office term signifying that a guest has departed but the room has to be cleaned and prepared for the new guest.

ONE-ARMED BANDIT - slot machine.

ONE BIG ONE - one thousand dollars.

ONE-DOWN - in craps, announcement by the stickperson that one die has fallen off the table.

ONE-EYED JACK - in poker, a term referring to when the jack of hearts and spades are used as wild cards.

ONE NUMBER BET - in craps, a bet that a specific number will or will not be thrown before another number.

ONE-ROLL BET - in craps, a term referring to a wager that will be decided on the next roll of the dice.

ON-LINE - a computer term referring to hardware that is capable of interacting directly with the central processing unit.

ON-THE-RAIL - a person who watches, but does not play, a game.

ON-THE-SQUARE - fair, honest.

ON-THE-STICK - in craps, a dealers' term referring to the rotation of dealers after a work break, when the new stickman begins the game or is "on the stick."

ON THE UP AND UP - straight, honest game.

ON THE WALL - a criminals term for the person who is assigned to be the lookout for approaching police.

OPEN - 1) in hotels, a term referring to the fact that rooms are still available, 2) in poker, the beginning bet of the game.

OPEN CRAPS - side bets among the players are permitted.

OPEN DOOR POLICY - employee problem resolution process where the workers can go directly to higher level managers.

OPEN ENDED QUESTIONS - in research, a term referring to the type of questions in which respondents are free to reply in their own words.

OPEN-END STRAIGHT - in poker, when the first four cards dealt are in numerical sequence and a fifth card is needed for the bottom or top to make a straight.

OPENER - 1) in poker, where the minimum hand needed to begin a poker pot is usually pair of jacks or better, 2) a casino term that refers to the slip of paper that is in the chip tray or check bank showing the amount of chip value for opening the game.

OPEN UP - 1) a casino term to start a game, 2) usually in a criminal context, a person who gives information or "opens up" with some pressure.

OPERANT CONDITIONING or INSTRUMENTAL CONDITIONING - a learning theory that views behavior as a reaction to a stimulus because of expected reinforcement. For example, Sally sees a slot machine at the end of the aisle, pulls the lever and receives ten dollars. The next time this situation happens, Sally will be likely to try again since she was rewarded with ten dollars the last time.

OPERATING COSTS - in management, money needed to pay the day to day expenses of a corporation.

OPINION LEADERS - people who are looked to for advice by others. For example, Sam wins at poker all the time so people ask him for suggestions on improving their game.

OPTIMIZATION MODELS - in economics, a statistical method for analyzing data by maximizing some criteria.

OPTION - choice of actions.

ORDINAL SCALE - in research term referring to the measurement of responses in which numbers are assigned on the basis of some order (one to five, best to worst).

ORGANIZATIONAL CULTURE - the pattern of beliefs and expectations shared by organizational members. For example, in the 1800's, the organizational culture in casinos was to obey the owner without any questions.

ORGANIZATIONAL STRUCTURE - in management, the formally designed framework of authority and task relationships in an organization.

ORGANIZATION CHART - in management, a term referring to the diagram of relationships between positions within an organization.

ORIENTATION - process of introducing a new employee to the job and organization.

OUTLIER - in research, a term referring to a response or data point that is radically different from the rest of the responses.

OUT-OF-ORDER or 000 - a guest room that cannot be used.

OUTSIDE - in roulette, the bets placed outside the table layout of the boxes for the thirty-seven or thirty-eight numbers.

OUT IN FRONT - when a player wins more than he/she loses.

OUTSIDE MAN - 1) a casino employee, pretending to be a player, who watches from outside the pit, 2) a non-casino employee, usually a cheat.

OUTSIDE WORK - a cheating term that refers to anything done to the surface of the dice.

OVERAGE - when the total of cash and checks in a register is greater than the initial bank plus net cash receipts.

OVERBOOKING - when a service organization accepts reservations that outnumber available units.

OVERHEAD - expenses that are needed to maintain the day to day functions of the firm.

OVERLAY - 1) in betting, a development when the odds are greater than they should be, 2) a player who bets more than his bankroll.

-P-

PACK - an unopened deck of fifty-two cards with two jokers.

PACKAGE - 1) a cheating term referring to a prestacked deck that is swapped for the actual playing cards, 2) in tourism, prepaid tour that includes transportation, lodging, and usually meals, transfers, sightseeing, or car rentals.

PACKAGE PLAN RATE - a special room rate that includes other meals, activities, or events.

PACK UP - to stop playing and leave the game.

PAD - 1) payroll, 2) the colored compartments of a roulette wheel.

PADDLE - the plastic slat that dealers use to push paper money into the drop box.

PAD ROLL - a cheating technique of throwing the dice so that they roll without spinning.

PAID-OUT - in lodging, an accounting term referring to the cash disbursed by the hotel on behalf of a guest and charged to the guest's account.

PAI-GOW - an oriental table game using thirty-two domino-type playing pieces and dice. There are seven players and a banker who each get a stack of four dominoes. The object of the game is to split the dominoes into two sets which have the highest possible ranking.

PAINT - a jack, queen, or king (sometimes a 10).

PAIR - 1) in European roulette, a bet on "Even", 2) in poker, a hand containing two cards of the same value.

PAIR-SPLITTING - in blackjack, a hand that contains two cards of the same value that can be split or separated and bet as two new separate hands.

PALM - a cheating technique that uses sleight of hand by picking up the cards from the table on a new deal and slipping the unwanted cards into the hollow of the palm of one's hand.

PAN - card game grouped under the generic name of "rummy".

PANHANDLER - a person who asks for money from players.

PAPER - 1) a cheating term referring to cards that are marked on the back, prior to play, 2) money.

PARIMUTUEL - races where all bets are pooled and the winner is paid off according to the number of winners, minus a standard track deduction.

PARITY - in management, a compensation term referring to the idea that each person who has responsibility to perform a task should have equivalent authority and/or pay to the others in similar jobs.

PARLAY - 1) a cumulative bet in which all monies won from one wager are automatically bet again, 2) to enlarge an original bankroll as in, he parlayed one hundred dollars into one thousand dollars.

PARTAGE or LE PARTAGE - in European roulette, there are two options for play when the ball lands on "0" or "00". The partage option means that the player simply divides the chips and keeps half.

PARTNERSHIP - a legal term referring to an unincorporated firm owned by two or more persons.

PARTY - a term used by cheats to signify opportunities for a scam.

PASS - 1) in craps, a bet that a shooter will throw a seven on the "come out" roll, 2) in craps, when a shooter wins a seven or eleven on the initial throw of the dice or makes his point on a subsequent roll.

PASSE - In European roulette, a bet on the high numbers, nineteen to thirty-six.

PASSERS - a cheating term referring to the crooked dice that tend to make more passes than fair dice.

PASS-LINE - 1) in craps, the area of layout of the table where the pass bets are made, 2) in craps, a basic wager where the player is betting with the shooter.

PAST-POSTING - an illegal practice of attempting to place a bet after the results are known.

PAT - a poker term referring to a hand that is good enough as it stands or the fact that no additional cards are needed for the hand, usually with a count of seventeen to twenty-one.

PATHOLOGICAL GAMBLING - according to the American Psychiatric Association it is an official mental disease or disorder, characterized by inability to stop wagering.

PAY - the compensation employees receive.

PAYOFF - 1) the collection of a bet, 2) any final event.

PAYOFF ODDS - ratio at which any bet is paid. For example, if one beats the dealer in blackjack, the payoff odds are one to one, which means that for every dollar bet, the player will receive a dollar return.

PAYOUT - in casinos, customer's winnings.

PAYOUT INTERVAL - how fast the player is paid. In casinos, payouts are immediate. However, in other forms of gambling, intervals vary. For example, a forty million dollar lottery can be paid over twenty years.

PAY THE BOARD - when the house elects to pay every player at the table, regardless of count total.

PBX - part of the communication's equipment, the hotel's telephone switchboard equipment.

P.C. - 1) a casino management term referring to the percentage of money put down the drop box and money given out of the rack to figure winnings and losses, 2) a casino term which relates to the percentage the house has as an advantage over the player.

P.C. DICE - in cheating equipment, crooked dice that give a cheat an advantage but do not win every time.

PEEK FREAK - disparaging term used by casino people to describe a hole card player.

PEEKING - a cheating technique where the thumb presses down and to the left of the top card, pushing it against the fingers on the opposite corner of the deck so that the top card buckles just enough for the dealer to get a glimpse of the inner corner of the card.

PEEK THE POKE - a cheater's term to describe the effort they must expend to determine how much cash is in a mark's wallet.

PEG - 1) in craps, indicates a point with a puck or marker on the number, 2) typecast a person.

PEGGING - using a small thumbtack, the cheater pricks certain cards in a spot. The idea is to "peg" the card without penetrating all the way through so that when dealing, the cheater can feel the cards.

PENCIL - a person having the juice (power) to write comps.

PENNY ANTE - wagers made for extremely small stakes.

PEPPER - an extremely "green" or naive victim of gambling cheats.

PERCEIVED RISK - how a person views the potential negative consequences of an action. For example, a habitual gambler will always acknowledge the money won and ignore the money lost, which allows him to continue hoping for the big jackpot. Therefore, he diminishes the perceived risk of losing, so that he can rationalize gambling.

PERCENTAGE - 1) house advantage expressed as a percentage, 2) in cheating, dice that alter the advantage.

PERCENTAGE GAME - a banking game in which an advantage is obtained through relatively disproportionate odds.

PERCENTAGE TOPS AND BOTTOMS - in cheating, a pair of altered, mis-spotted, dice that usually have a deuce or a five twice on the die.

PERCEPTION - a psychological term referring to the process by which stimuli are selected, organized and interpreted. For example, gamblers who see themselves as lucky may only perceive the wins and not the loses. This is a perceptual distortion.

PERFECTS - casino quality dice that are perfect cubes to a tolerance of 1/5,000 of an inch.

PERFORMANCE - a management term referring to the process of expending effort to reach individual or organizational goals.

PERFORMANCE APPRAISAL - a management term referring to the review of employee job performance in relation to job standards and expectations.

PERFORMANCE FEEDBACK - a management communication tool to give evaluative information about an employee's progress toward a specific goal.

PERSONALITY - a person's psychological makeup which influences his/her reactions to the environment. For example, security people who sit in a room alone and watch the monitors for eight hours should not be people who are "social animals". Therefore the personality traits for a security monitor person would be a solitary person who pays a great deal of attention to details.

PERSONAL SELLING - a marketing tool used in person to person communication.

PERSUASION - a psychological weapon that is an active attempt to change a person's attitude.

PHILISTINES - loan sharks.

PHOEBE - in craps, the point five.

PHONY - 1) in cheating, crooked dice, 2) describing a person who is a fake.

PHYSICAL DISTRIBUTION - a marketing term referring to the process of physically moving goods from source of supply to point of consumption.

PIA - 1) an acronym for "paid in advance," 2) a hotelier's term for a guest who pays in cash during registration.

PICK-AND-PAY - a dealer's method of turning over a player's cards, paying, or taking the bets, and picking up that hand before proceeding to the next player's hand.

PICTURE CARDS - in a deck of cards, the face cards (jack, queen, king).

PIECE - a slang term for a share of the profits.

PIECE OF CAKE - an expression referring to a simple, easy, or pleasant job.

PIGEON - a cheater's jargon for a victim in a gambling scam.

PIKER - a gambler who makes small bets opposite big bettors because the bank will beat the big player.

PIMS or PROFIT IMPACT ON MARKET SHARE - a strategic marketing process that gathers data from a number of corporations to establish a relationship between a variety of business factors and measure organizational performance.

PINCH - a casino term referring to the instance when a person tries to illegally remove part, or all, of a wager.

PINCH AND PRESS - a cheating technique where a player adds or subtracts from his bet after seeing his cards.

PINCHING - increasing or decreasing a bet after completion of play.

PIPS - a cheating scam where the design on the cards indicates its denomination.

PIT - in the casino layout, a single grouping of adjacent table games.

PIT BOSS - in the casino management hierarchy, the most senior gaming supervisor in the pit (grouping of tables) who supervises play and the activities of several floorpersons.

PIT-STAND - the desk stand for floorpersons' use in writing or phoning while they are in the pit.

PIZZA - in baccarat, a random method of mixing cards prior to shuffling.

PLACE BET - in craps, a bet on the result of a throw when the shooter is trying for a point.

PLAY - a casino term referring to the betting or action.

PLAYER - a casino term referring to the gambler, bettor, or patron.

PLAYER HAND - in baccarat, one of the two betting propositions.

PLAYER'S ADVANTAGE - a gambling term referring to the percent of money bet that a player can expect to win in the long run.

PLAYER'S BIAS - a casino term referring to the bias in the ordering of deck or shoe of cards when it favors the player.

PLEASURE PRINCIPLE - a psychological theory that says a person's behavior is motivated by the desire to maximize pleasure and avoid pain.

PLUS COUNT - in card counting for blackjack, when the counter believes that there is an excess of ten value cards in proportion to low value cards.

POCKET - in roulette, a part of the equipment that refers to the compartments on the roulette wheel where the ball falls.

POINT - in craps play, where a shooter tries to throw the dice so that a four, five six, eight, nine, or ten on the come-out roll and then tries to roll the same number before throwing a seven.

POINT BET - in craps, a bet whether or not the point will be made.

POINT COUNT - in card counter's terms for blackjack, the player's evaluation of the odds via a tally of assigned points of each card.

POINT NUMBERS - in craps, a four, five, six, eight, nine, or ten.

POINT OF PURCHASE DISPLAYS - a marketing term referring to the promotional materials that attempt to influence a consumers' or players' decisions at the time of purchase.

POINT SPREAD - a handicap in the form of points added by odds-makers to the scores of teams in games of predictable outcomes that are the object of betting.

POKE - wallet.

POKER - a card game where the objective is to win the pot by either exposing the best hand at the final showdown, or by being the last player left in the hand which happens when a player forces the other players out by making a final bet that no other player calls.

POLICY - in management, a statement used as a decision making guide to implement a strategic plan.

POLLY - politician.

PONTOON - another name for blackjack, twenty-one, or the French vingt-et-un.

POPULATION - a research term referring to all of the possibilities in a selected group.

PORTFOLIO ANALYSIS - a marketing analysis as to which markets or products should be maintained, expanded, or phased out.

POSITIONING - a marketing term referring to the fit of a product to a segment of the market so that it is perceived as different from the competition.

POSITIVE DECK - a card counter's term referring to when the remaining cards in the deck have a favorable plus count.

POSITIVE REINFORCEMENT - a psychological learning term referring to the fact that rewards provided by the environment strengthen responses to the stimuli. For example, slot machines provide intermittent positive reinforcements in the form of pay outs so that people will bet more.

POSTING - a hotel term referring to the process of recording transactions on a guest folio.

POUND - five dollars.

POT - total money or chips in a pool to be taken by the winning player(s).

POWER - potential to influence the behavior of others.

PREFERENTIAL - a casino move to break up a positive count for a card counter where the dealer shuffles the deck.

PREMIUM - a pricing term that is an offer of an item or service either free, or at a low price, as an extra incentive for purchasers.

PREMIUM HOUSE - a casino that caters to "high rollers" or people who habitually bet a lot of money.

PREMIUM PLAYER - a casino term referring to a person who consistently bets high stakes, commonly called a "high roller".

PRE-REGISTRATION - in lodging, a process where parts of the registration are completed before the guest arrives.

72

PRESENT VALUE - a financial term referring to today's value for assets that yield a stream of income over time.

PRESS - a gambling term referring to doubling a bet.

PRESS-A-BET - a gambling term referring to increasing a bet after a win.

PRESS RELEASE - a marketing term referring to the factual information released to the press.

PRESTIGE PRICING - a marketing term referring to the practice of pricing a product high so that a consumer will perceive quality and status.

PREVENTIVE MAINTENANCE - in the engineering department, maintenance should be performed at regularly scheduled intervals to minimize equipment failure and prolong the operating life of equipment.

PRICE - 1) in casino marketing, a term denoted by the percentage of the gross amount wagered (handle) retained by the operators and is equivalent to the losses incurred by all gamblers over a period of time, 2) the value a willing buyer will exchange for goods or services.

PRICE ELASTICITY - an economic term quantifying the degree to which quantity demanded by buyers responds to a price change.

PRICE FLEXIBILITY - an economic term describing the market condition when the immediate price change depends on changes in supply or demand. For example, auctions.

PRICE INDEX - an economic term used by the government or industry to evaluate the average price of a bundle of goods so that prices can be compared over time.

PRIMARY DATA - a research term describing the information collected for the express purpose of answering the question at hand.

PROBABILITY - a statistics term describing the likelihood that one among a number of possible outcomes of an event will occur.

PROBABILITY SAMPLE - a research term describing that each subject in the population has an equal chance of being selected.

PROCEDURE - casino management policies or guides for performing planned activities that occur regularly.

PRODUCT DIFFERENTIATION - a marketing term evaluating the characteristics that make a product different from its competitors.

PRODUCTION FUNCTION - an economic term specifying the amount of output that can be achieved with given inputs.

PRODUCTIVITY - a management term referring to the ratio of output to inputs.

PRODUCT POSITIONING - a marketing term describing the traits that allow the product to meet a customer's perceived needs while separating it from competitors.

PROFIT - an accounting term quantified as sales revenue minus costs, properly chargeable against the goods sold.

PROFIT CENTER - a strategic management term for a highly autonomous unit given broad decision making authority for its own operations.

PROFIT SHARING - a compensation program where certain employees can receive a portion of organizational profits.

PROGRESSION - a betting sequence where the player gambles an incremental increase in the wager after decisions.

PROMOTION - a strategic marketing process to coordinate seller-initiated efforts to set up channels of information and persuasion to sell services or to promote an idea.

PROPERTY MANAGEMENT SYSTEM or PMS - a hotel term for the computer software that supports front office and back office activities.

PROPOSITION BETS - in craps, a bet on long shots.

PROSPECT - potential buyer.

PSYCHOGRAPHICS - a strategic marketing term referring to the use of psychological and sociological factors to develop groups of people with common interests. For example, the MGM Grand in Las Vegas used psychographic information about families to develop a themed amusement park.

PUBLICITY - a marketing communications term that refers to the press coverage that is not paid directly to the media and is not controlled by the corporation.

PUCK - part of the craps table equipment that is a marker used to indicate the point number and whether odds are on or off on the come-out roll.

PULL DOWN - in craps, when a player takes back all or part of a wager just won rather than let it continue for the next roll.

PULL UP - a scam artist's term for a possible mark who loses interest.

PULL UP A PLAY - a cheat signal between partners calling a play in counting or hole card action.

PUNCHY - mentally slow.

PUNK - 1) slang term referring to a novice, 2) slang term referring to a small time gambler or crook.

PUNTO BANCO - a table game also known as Baccarat, Chemin de fer, American Baccarat, Nevada Baccarat.

PURSE DRAWER - the bottom part of the casino table where a drawer is located that holds the table accessories and dealer's purse.

PUSH - a standoff or tie between the player and the dealer where neither wins or loses.

PUT ON THE SEND - a scam artist's term referring to sending a mark home to get more money.

PUT-UP - a gambling term referring to the situation where a player makes a bet on behalf of the dealer.

PUT THE BITE ON - slang term referring to someone who wants to borrow money.

PUT THE FINGER ON - a slang term referring to identifying criminals to the police in secret.

PUT THE HORNS ON - slang for a bad luck omen to a player.

PUT-THE-LID-ON - when a casino closes a table by covering the rack with a locked lid.

PUT THE PRESSURE ON - coercion.

-Q-

QUALITY CIRCLES - a management practice where work groups meet regularly to discuss, investigate, and correct quality problems.

QUALITY OF LIFE - a sociological term referring to an emphasis on the relationships and concern for others that indicate how happy people are with their lives.

QUARTERS - twenty-five dollar table checks.

QUEER - 1) slang for counterfeit money, 2) a slang term for upsetting someone's plans.

QUEUING MODELS - a mathematical analysis of the costs of waiting lines.

QUINELLA - used in racing, when the bettor must pick the first two horses that cross the finish line.

-R-

RABBIT - 1) a person who scares easily, 2) a sucker.

RACK - a piece of equipment for the tables which is a rectangular metal tray which contains the table checks and silver, and lies flat in the middle of table next to the dealer.

RACK RATE - a hotel term which refers to the standard or full-price rates established by the property.

RAFFLE - a lottery.

RAIL - 1) a casino term referring to the carpeted area bordering the gaming tables, 2) in roulette, the wheel groove where the ball spins.

RAIL-BIRD - a thief who steals unaware players' gaming chips from the edge, or "rail", of the table.

RAISE - in poker, when a player bets more than the previous player and forces all opponents to match the higher stakes or drop out of the game.

RAKE - croupier's stick.

RANDOM DISTRIBUTION - a mathematical probability where everything has an equal opportunity to be selected.

RANK - the face value of a card.

RAT HOLE - a cheater's place to hide illegally obtained chips or money.

RATING - a casino term referring to the measure of a player's potential value as a casino customer for the purpose of allocating complimentaries.

RATING SLIP - 1) a sheet which indicates a player's activity for comps, 2) a record of a dealer's performance.

RATIO ANALYSIS - financial data expressed in the form of a comparison in order to evaluate organizational performance.

RATS - dice.

READABLE DEALER - a casino term for a dealer whose hole card can be spotted by a person in casino.

READERS - a cheater's glasses or lenses to read marked cards.

READY A TRAY - a casino term referring to the way the dealers' organize the tray so that a supervisor can count the content of the chip tray from a distance.

READY UP - prepare.

REAL DOUGH - large quantity of money.

REAL INCOME - in economics, income that is adjusted for inflation.

REAL WORK - a cheater's slang for genuine inside information of the correct way to perform a cheating move or scam.

RECRUITMENT - an organization's efforts to generate a list of job applicants.

RED - in roulette, a bet paying one to one.

REDS - five dollar table cheques or chips.

RED-DOG - a casino table game in which players bet that the third card drawn will fall between the values of two previously drawn cards.

REEL STRIP SETTINGS - in casinos, the payout percentages which are pre-set in the slot machines.

REEL TIMING - in slots, a player's attempt to time the spin of the reels and set them in motion so that they will come to rest in desired positions.

REFERENCE GROUPS - in consumer behavior, groups that set behavior standards to which other individuals adhere.

REGISTRATION - the procedure when an incoming guest signs the forms to contract for their stay.

REGULATION - the government laws or rules designed to change the behavior of firms or organizations.

RELAY - a person who transmits signals from one person to another in a casino.

RELIABILITY - 1) a research design question referring to the likelihood that the results can be duplicated again, with similar results, 2) the way a product or service fulfills its intended function.

RELIEF-DEALER - a casino term referring to the new dealer who takes the place of the table dealer for break.

RENEGE - refuse to pay a wager or debt.

RESEARCH DESIGN - plan for a study that guides the collection and analysis of the data.

RESEARCH PROCESS - a sequence of steps in the design and implementation of an experiment.

RESERVATION - an agreement between a guest and a business to hold a specific type of room or table for a date and length of time.

RESOURCES - a strategic management term referring to the organization's people, capital, technology, clients, and time.

RE-SPIN - 1) in roulette, where the ball rolls on the wheel, 2) on a big six wheel, when the clapper stops on top of a peg, a second spin occurs.

RESPONSIBILITIES - an employee's assigned tasks, duties, and obligations to achieve expected performance results.

RESTRUCTURING - a strategic management term referring to alterations in the organizational chart for more efficient distribution of resources.

RETAIL - a type of business that involves the majority of the sale of goods and services directly to consumers for their personal, family, or household use.

RETURN - in gambling, the percentage of total money that is paid out to the customers.

RETURN ON ASSETS or ROA - a financial performance ratio based on a net sales, net profits, and total assets.

RETURN ON INVESTMENT or ROI - a financial ratio that compares net income to stockholders' equity.

REVENUE - 1) a financial term referring to the money earned by a business operation or income, 2) from the casino point of view, collective losses of gamblers.

REVOLUTIONS - a casino term referring to when a wheel or reel spins one complete circle back to the start.

REWARD POWER - a management term referring to the ability of a manager to distribute bonuses.

RFB - a casino term for the ultimate comp - free room, meals, and drinks.

RHYTHM PLAY - in playing slot machines, the method used by players to attempt to control the combinations by carefully timing the pull of the handle.

RICH - a card counter's term referring to a shoe with a larger than normal percentage of a certain value of cards present.

RIEN NE VA PLUS - in roulette, the croupier's call that ends betting on one spin of the wheel.

RIFFLE - a dealer's term referring to a method of shuffling cards by dividing the deck in two and intermingling the two sections.

RIG - a cheating maneuver to fix or prearrange a game's outcome.

RIGHT-BETTOR - in craps, when a player bets the shooter will make his point.

RIP - a cheating maneuver to switch dice.

RIP AND TEAR - to cheat without fear of the consequences.

RIPE - 1) ready to make a loan, 2) novice primed to be taken.

RISK - conditions where the decision maker has to estimate the likelihood of certain outcomes.

RISK OF RUIN - the probability that the gambler will tap out or lose the entire bankroll within a defined period or before achieving a specified goal.

RIVERBOAT - a type of casino that floats on water.

ROAD HUSTLER - a cheat who travels around looking for a game.

ROCK - a player who refuses to lend money.

ROD - handgun.

ROLE - a sociological term referring to a set of behavior patterns expected of someone occupying a given position in a social unit. For example, the role of the breadwinner of a family is to bring home the money.

ROLL - 1) a criminal move to steal from a person while they're asleep or intoxicated, 2) in craps, the throwing of the dice.

ROLLER - 1) in cards, the weight that holds the cards against the shoe, 2) player or gambler.

ROLLING FULL BLOOM - fast paced, high stakes game.

ROLLING-THE-BONES - a player's term for shooting craps.

ROLL OVER - 1) slang for a criminal partner who tells the police what they know, 2) in accounting, when an investment like a CD comes due, and it is automatically reinvested, 3) in casino accounting, paying off old markers with newly issued credit instruments.

ROOMS DIVISION - a hotel department that includes the front office, reservations, telephone switchboard, housekeeping, uniformed service departments and functions.

ROPE - cheat.

ROPE IN - a scam artist's term for luring a mark into a swindle.

ROPER - a hustler who recruits victims for gambling scams.

ROSCOE - handgun.

ROTATION - the direction a wheel is spun.

ROUGE - in roulette, a bet on red.

ROUGE ET NOIR - French casino game also called Trente et Quarante or thirty and forty.

ROUGH IT UP - a gambling term to bet heavily.

ROULETTE - a casino table game in which players bet on one or a combination of thirty-eight numbers, where a small white ball is spun against a horizontal rotating wheel and where it lands on the winning number.

ROYAL FLUSH - in poker, the highest possible hand which includes a ten, jack, queen, king and ace, all in the same suit.

RUBBER-BAND - a management system of assigning dealers to table games after the break, when the dealers are not assigned a specific table.

RUG JOINT - a plush gambling house.

RULE - an explicit statement that dictates what is acceptable.

RUMBLE - to discover crooked dealings.

RUN - length of time.

RUN-DOWN - small, regulation-sized, stacks of cheques, easily counted from a distance.

RUNNERS - in keno, the casino personnel who pick up a customer's ticket and wager from anywhere in the casino hotel and take it to the Keno booth.

RUNNING-COUNT - a card counter's cumulative value of all cards played at any given time, based on a preassigned values for each card.

RUN OF THE HOUSE - a hotel term to guarantee a firm price that applies to any room in the house.

RUNT - in poker, a hand of less than one pair.

-S-

SABOT - a piece of equipment of table games called a dealing shoe.

SALARY - an accounting term referring to a consistent payment for work rendered.

SALES PROMOTION -a paid marketing communication that stimulates short term consumer purchases.

SALLE PRIVEE - In Europe, a private salon in the casino reserved for high stakes games.

SAND WORK - a cheaters' method of marking the backs of cards with very fine sandpaper.

SATISFICING - a type of management decision process where the adopted decision that meets previously established minimum criteria, even when further search might reveal a better alternative.

SAWBUCK - ten dollars.

SAWDUST-JOINT - low budget or low roller casino.

SCALAR PRINCIPLE - concept that organizations should have a chain of authority and communication that runs from top to bottom and that should be followed by managers and subordinates.

SCAM - a method for cheating a gambling opponent.

SCORE - 1) a dealer's term for a bigger than normal tip night, 2) in general, a gambler's term for winning big, 3) in craps, to win, 4) slang term for buying illegal drugs, 5) a cheater's term for the proceeds of a con game.

SCORE A BIG TOUCH - to cheat a player out of a large amount of money.

SCRATCH - 1) money, 2) in blackjack, the scraping motion of the cards a player uses to request a "hit" or take another card.

SDS SYSTEM - a computerized slot tracking system where the player inserts a plastic card into a "reader" in order to record how long he/she plays and how much money he/she deposits into the machine in order to get credit for his/her playing time.

SEAT OF THE PANTS - slang for making decisions based on intuition.

SEASONAL VARIATIONS - a management term referring to the fluctuations of a variable that occur regularly during a yearly cycle.

SECOND BASE - in a table game, the name of the position of the player sitting near the center of the table.

SECONDS - a cheating move when a dealer does not deal the top cards from the deck.

SECONDARY DATA - a statistical term referring to information that is not gathered for the immediate study at hand but for some other purpose.

SECURITY - 1) casino "police", 2) the department that controls and protects the casino from crimes, 3) protection of all people who are legitimately on the firm's property, from bodily harm caused by the deliberate behavior of another person.

SECURITY MONITOR - a closed circuit television monitor that allows employees to monitor security and safety throughout the property from a central location.

SELF-ACTUALIZATION - a psychological term referring to reaching one's ultimate potential through the use of personal skills and creative talents.

SELF-CONCEPT - a psychological term referring to the attitude a person holds toward him or herself. For example, a person with a great deal of confidence in his abilities will be more likely to try new games such as moving from slots to the tables.

SELF-ESTEEM NEEDS - a psychological term referring to a motivational need to feel good about oneself.

SENIORITY - a term that refers to how long a person has been working for the company.

SENSOR - a device that senses a specific change in its environment and transmits a signal, so that some predetermined action can take place. For example, a motion sensor can be used to detect any action in the money vault.

SENT IT IN - a gambling term referring to a bet against the house for large and/or frequent amounts of money.

SEQUENCE - 1) in card playing, the order of rank in the cards, 2) in general, any chain of events and consequences.

SERVICE - a type of product that is intangible, goods that are inseparable from the provider, variable in quality, and perishable.

SEVEN-OUT - in craps, rolling a seven after the initial throw, which becomes the shooter's losing point.

SEXUAL HARASSMENT - a legal term referring to behavior marked by sexually suggestive remarks, unwanted touching and sexual advances, requests for sexual favors, or other verbal or physical conduct of a sexual nature.

SHADE - a con artist's term for a cover or distraction for a scam.

SHAPE - a cheating technique that cuts down the die.

SHAPING BEHAVIOR - a psychological term referring to systematically reinforcing each successive step that moves an individual closer to the desired response. For example, a person riding a bus to the casino is rewarded for getting on the bus with free twenty dollar chips; he puts the chips in the slot machine and is rewarded with a payout; he puts his own money in and is rewarded with a payout.

SHARK - 1) any money loaner who charges exorbitant fees, 2) a skilled shooter who cheats.

SHARP - 1) confident person, 2) dapper or decked out in sartorial splendor.

SHARPER - a card cheat or superior player who takes advantage of novices.

SHAKE OUTS - in competitive life cycles, in a growing market place many competitors join in, however once the market has been saturated, a shake out occurs which is when many weaker competitors drop out.

SHAVED - a cheater's term for trimmed or altered dice.

SHELL - an engineering term for the basic structural elements of a building, including the outside and supporting walls, foundation, frame, and roof.

SHIELD - in roulette, the glass surrounding the wheel that protects the public from flying balls.

SHIFT - eight hour work day.

SHIFT-BOSS - in the casino management hierarchy, the person who controls the entire casino on his shift and answers only to the casino manager.

SHILL - a casino term for an employee who sits down at an empty table and acts as a player to help get the game started.

SHINER - a cheater's device referring to a small mirror which reflects the face of the top card of the deck as it is dealt.

SHOE - in baccarat and blackjack, the container which stores the undealt cards.

SHOT - an illegal move by a player.

SHOOT - in craps, a completed round in which the shooter makes or fails to make the point.

SHOOTER - in craps, a term referring to the player who is throwing the dice.

SHOOTING FROM THE HIP - a slang expression referring to making a decision spontaneously.

SHORTAGE - an accounting term referring to when the total of cash and checks in the cash register drawer is less than the initial bank plus net cash receipts.

SHORTCAKE - short change.

SHORT HORN - in craps, small bet on the horn.

SHORT SHOE - in blackjack, the shoe with a number of cards removed from the decks used. This alters the percentage against the players.

SHOWDOWN - in poker, after all bets are made, revealing the final hand.

SHUFFLE - in card games, the randomizing process of the cards before play starts.

SHUFFLE TRACKING - in card games, the process where a card player seeks to follow certain cards as they are shuffled in order to identify when they are likely to appear in the reshuffled deck.

SHY - 1) a slang term for owing money, 2) a slang term for short on cash.

SHYLOCK - an individual who loans money to players who have gone broke.

SHYSTER - inexpensive, unscrupulous lawyer.

SIC-BO - oriental table game played with three dice. The objective is to select the individual numbers, or combination of numbers, that appear on the dice after they are shaken in a cup and exposed by the house dealer.

SIDE BET - in craps, a bet made between players or onlookers for the results of a particular throw of the dice.

SIDE GAME - a casino term for a less important and relatively lightly played game in a casino.

SILVER - silver dollars or one dollar gaming tokens.

SILVER TONGUE - 1) high-class conman, 2) convincing talker.

SINGLE-DECK - a blackjack game played with one deck (52 cards) and almost always hand-held by the dealer.

SINGLE-0 - 1) a conman's term for working alone, 2) in roulette, the single zero on the wheel.

SINGLES - one dollar checks.

SIX-ACE FLATS - a gambling term for a pair of corrupted dice.

SIXAINE -in roulette, the term for a six number bet (two horizontal rows with three numbers each).

SIXTY DAYS - in craps, the six point.

SIZE-INTO - a quick way of accounting at the table where the dealers push a stack of cheques up to a shorter stack of cheques and take the excess off, so both stacks are equal.

SKIMMING - in embezzling, altering the accounting so that sums of money can be illegally taken "off the top" without knowledge.

SKINNER - a cheat.

SKINNY DUGAN - in craps, a loser seven.

SKY - 1) a security term referring to the area above the main casino where play is observed through one-way mirrors and video equipment, 2) a casino term referring to the employee(s) assigned to work in the "sky" area. This is short for eye-in-the-sky or casino surveillance.

SLAMBANG - a gambling term for heavy, quick action.

SLEEPER - 1) a gambling term referring to an unclaimed bet, wager or part of a wager forgotten by player, 2) a gambling term referring to a number that has not come up for a very long time.

SLICK CUP - a cheater's tool that is a dice cup with a polished inside surface to facilitate the effectiveness of loaded dice.

SLICK DICE - a cheater's dice that have been altered to have smooth sides and rough sides.

SLICKERS - professional gamblers.

SLIDE SHOT -a dice mechanic's technique for controlling the roll of one or two dice.

SLOT DROP - in casinos, the amount of coins collected in the bucket inside a cabinet underneath the slot machine.

SLOT HANDLE - in casinos, amount of money deposited into the machine by the customer.

SLOTS - an abbreviation for slot machines which are the mechanical, computerized game machines.

SLOW PLAY - in poker, a strategic technique of placing a small bet as an opener, then if challenged, coming back with a large re-raise.

SLUG - 1) in slot play, a cheater's false coin or chip, 2) in cards, a group of cards arranged by cheats for a desired result, 3) a cheater's device of a metal weight used to load dice.

SMACKER - 1) one dollar, 2) a stupid person.

SMART - a gambler's term referring to someone who knows the score.

SMART MONEY - an intelligent gambler.

SNAKE-EYES - in craps, a throw of two aces (ones).

SNAPPER - 1) in blackjack, a hand where the first two cards are an ace and ten count, and pays one and a half times the bet, 2) a slang term for blackjack.

SOCIAL CLASS - a sociological term referring to the relatively homogeneous divisions of society into which people are grouped based on similar lifestyles, values, norms, interests, and behaviors. For example, a casino that attracts the lower social class is more likely to have a majority of nickel slot machines rather than baccarat tables.

SOCIAL NEEDS - a psychological term referring to the motivational requirements that people have social interaction.

SOCIAL RESPONSIBILITY - a term referring to the organization's obligation to be aware of its impact on the surrounding environment and to take appropriate actions.

SOFT - easy.

SOFT COUNT - in casinos, counting the value of paper like dollar bills, cheques, markers, etc.

SOFT-HAND - in blackjack, a hand with an ace which can be valued as one or eleven.

SOFT OPENING - in hotels and other similar facilities, when the property opens for business prior to the "official opening" in order to smooth out operations.

SOLID - trustworthy, good.

SOVEREIGN NATION - in Native American tribes, a federal status indicating that they are a separate body from Americans and as such, they are exempt from state betting limits or taxation.

SPA - a type of hotel or resort that provides hot springs, baths, or other health and fitness facilities, and services.

SPAN OF CONTROL - a management term referring to the number of subordinates reporting directly to a superior.

SPECIFICATIONS - an engineering term referring to the descriptions and directions that accompany blueprints.

SPELL - in craps, a term referring to a similar sequence of passes.

SPIN - in roulette, a term referring to setting the wheel in play.

SPINDLE - in roulette, a metal piece which attaches the roulette wheel to the hub.

SPIN THEM - in craps, an attempt to control the dice.

SPIT - gambling term referring to a player's very small bankroll.

SPLASH MOVE - ploy by gambling cheats who run through a cheating method without actually doing it, to see if any suspicions are aroused.

SPLINTERS - individual player, arriving independently or on a junket, who are brought in by the casino to gamble.

SPLIT - in blackjack, a pair which can be split into two hands as long as the same amount is bet on each hand. A player who splits, draws cards for both hands.

SPLIT BET - bet on two numbers.

SPLITTER - a cheater's term referring to a substitute gaffed die which is interchanged for one of a pair of crooked dice to change the outcome.

SPLITTING PAIRS - in blackjack, when two of a kind can be turned into two separate hands.

SPOOK - a cheating term referring to a person who reads the dealer's hole card.

SPOOKING - a cheating maneuver where a team of cheats read the dealer's hole card and bet accordingly.

SPOONING - in slot machines, a cheating device that is spoon-shaped and used to bring about a payoff.

SPOT - slang term referring to someone who discovers a deviation.

SPOTS - 1) the area printed on the felt layout designating where the bets are to be placed, 2) in keno, the numbers a player marks on a card.

SPREAD - when a player bets more than one hand simultaneously.

SPREADSHEET - a software package that allows the user to turn a computer's memory into a large worksheet in which data and formulas can be entered to perform a variety of calculations.

SPREAD-YOUR-DECK - a casino expression referring to a dealer gathering up all the cards and spreading them in a smooth arc in the middle of the table.

SPRING - 1) slang for getting a person released from police custody, 2) a slang expression for someone to pick up the tab.

SQUARE - 1) in roulette, a bet on four connected numbers 2) a slang expression for a conservative individual who is not in fashion.

SQUARE A BEEF - a slang expression which means to resolve a gripe.

SQUARE IT - a slang expression where a person corrects a wrong.

SQUARES - any honest gambling equipment.

SQUAWKER - loud, habitual complainer.

SQUEEZE - 1) cheating device, 2) control, coerce.

STACK - a column of twenty cheques or coins.

STACKED DECK - a cheating term that refers to a pack of cards that have been prearranged to suit a specific purpose.

STAKE - 1) a wager, 2) the money to be bet on a series of gambles.

STAKEHOLDERS - a management term referring to any constituency in the environment that is affected by an organization's decision and policies. For example, two types of stakeholders for a casino can be the employees and stockholders.

STAKES - a gambling term referring to the amount wagered.

STAND - a blackjack term referring to a player's decision not to draw additional cards.

STAND ALONE - a management term for something that can be separated from the whole and still function efficiently. For example, a hotel can be a "stand alone" division or it can be used as part of the casino effort as an amenity.

STANDARD HOURS - a management term referring to the amount of time in which a given, well defined, procedure should be accomplished.

STANDARD OPERATING PROCEDURES or SOP - a management term referring to the traditional ways operations are done, often dictated by the corporate headquarters.

STANDARDS - levels of expected performance.

STAND-UP PERSON - trustworthy.

STANDARD DEVIATION - a mathematical concept referring to the spread of results around an expected point.

STANDOFF - a tie.

STATUS SYMBOL - in consumer behavior, tangible evidence of an individual's social position.

STAY - a player's indication to the dealer that no more cards are desired on a hand.

STEAM - heavy surveillance.

STEAMING - a player's strategy of increasing the bet after each losing hand during a losing streak.

STEAMER - a player on a losing streak, who increases the size of his bets in an effort to recoup his losses.

STEER JOINT - crooked casino.

STEERER - a scam artist who finds suckers to come to a steer joint.

STEREOTYPING - a psychological term referring to the tendency to judge a person on the basis of one's perception of a group, like race or age.

STICK - in craps, the hockey stick-like device the dealer uses to retrieve the dice from across the table to return them to the shooter.

STICKMAN - in craps, the dealer, who stands directly across from the boxman, calls the game and controls its pace. He uses a hooked stick to retrieve the dice and push them toward the shooter.

STIFF - 1) a gambling term referring to a winning gambler who doesn't toke (tip) the dealer, 2) in blackjack, a hand that has a small chance of winning (12-16 points), 3) someone who does not bet for dealers.

STIFFED - slang for a person who receives no tip for providing services like a dealer or a server.

STIFF HAND - in blackjack, a difficult hand which has a total of twelve to sixteen and may bust if an additional card is drawn.

STING - a cheater's term for when the conman gets the money.

STOCK - a casino term referring to the portion of an undealt deck of cards that may be used later during the same deal.

STONEWALL JACKSON - miser.

STORE - slang term for a casino.

STORE DICE - imperfect cubes or dice.

STORM - a gamblers term for a statistically significant deviation from the average.

STRADDLE - in poker, a bet of twice the ante placed by the second player before the deal.

STRAIGHT - in poker, a hand of any five cards in numerical sequence.

"STRAIGHTEN-UP-YOUR-RACK" - a casino expression said to a dealer indicating that they should arrange the racked silver and cheques into regulation stacks so that the floorperson can quickly count from a distance.

STRAIGHT-FLUSH - in poker, any five cards in numerical sequence and the same suit.

STRAIGHT-TICKET - in keno, a simple ticket with no combination bets.

STRAIGHT UP BET - in roulette, a bet on a single number.

STRATEGIC BUSINESS UNITS or SBU - a management term referring to a structural group within a firm that has some autonomy.

STREAK - a gambling term referring to a series of wins or losses.

STREET BET - in roulette, a bet on a row of three numbers across.

STRESS - a generic term referring to the mobilization of the body's energy sources when confronted with demands or conflict.

STRIKE NUMBER - for card counters, the strategic number that alters the betting.

STRINGING - in slots, a cheating technique where a cheat inserts a coin on a string and pulls it back up out of the machine.

STRIP - a universal term for the casino row along Las Vegas Boulevard (Las Vegas Strip).

STRIPPERS - a cheater's device which refers to a deck of cards whose edges have been trimmed.

93

STRIP- THE- DECK - a cheating method of shuffling which consists of dropping a few cards at a time off the top of the deck.

STRONG - effective cheating move.

STRONG ARM - physical coercion.

STUCK - lose.

STUD-POKER - in poker, a game in which some of the cards are dealt face up and others face down.

STUFFED - person with plenty of cash.

SUB - a cheating technique in which a concealed pocket or other device on the clothing or body is used for holding illegally taken cheques.

SUCKER - gullible.

SUCKER BET - a gambling term referring to a bet that has a high probability of losing.

SUCKER WORD - cheating terms used only by non-cheaters.

SUCTION DICE - dice with concave surfaces.

SUITE - in a hotel, one or more bedrooms connected to a parlor or living room.

SUITE HOTEL - a type of hotel whose guestrooms have a separate bedroom and living spaces and sometimes a kitchenette.

SUPER GEORGE - in dealer's jargon, a player who bets a lot for the dealer.

SURE THING - any bet that has very little chance of losing.

SURRENDER - in blackjack, to give up on a bad hand and lose half the bet.

SURVEILLANCE - the ability of the organization to observe all behaviors on the total area of the property.

SURVEY - a research tool where information is systematically gathered.

SWEATER - a casino term for a person who only watches a game.

SWEEP - a casino term for clearing the chips off the table.

SWINGING - a casino term for stealing by a casino employee.

SWITCH - a con technique for illegally exchanging one article for another.

SWOT - a strategic planning term for the analysis of an organization's strengths and weaknesses against the environmental opportunities and threats.

SYSTEM - any strategic method using a mathematical calculation of chances.

SYSTEMS APPROACH - a management theory that sees an organization as a set of interrelated and interdependent parts.

-T-

TABLE BANKROLL - in blackjack, the chips in the tray at a specific table.

TABLE DROP - 1) in casinos, the amount of money, and markers, that is placed into the drop box at a gaming table, 2) in casinos, the amount of money that a customer exchanges, cash for chips.

TABLE GAME - a game that uses a table as part of the action.

TABLE HOPPING - a gambling term for a person who switches gaming tables in an attempt to change one's luck.

TABLE LIMIT - a casino term for the maximum and minimum bets allowed at a table.

TABLE WIN - in casinos, this amount is calculated by subtracting the value of the chips missing from the bankroll of the table from the drop.

T-ACCOUNT - in accounting, a two-column system where charges are posted on the left side and payments on the right side.

TAKE - 1) a gaming expression for the casino receipts, 2) slang for accepting a bribe, 3) depart.

TAKE AND PAY - a casino term referring to the dealer's method of settling up with the winners and losers.

TAKE AN EDGE - in gaming, to acquire a dishonest advantage.

TAKE-DOWN - in gaming, to remove a bet (usually pertains to a bet for the dealers.)

TAKE IT -a craps term for backing the dice to win by taking the odds.

TAKE IT OFF FROM THE INSIDE - employee theft.

TAKE IT OFF THE TOP - a payout before any disbursements are made.

TAKE-ME-DOWN - in craps, an instruction from a player to the dealer meaning "remove my bet(s)."

TAKE OFF MAN - partner from a cheating scam who makes the large wagers.

TAKE OFF PAD - place at the front base of the shoe where the cards are drawn.

TAKE THE ODDS - in craps, to accept a "wrong" bet at odds.

TAKING THE COUNT - in casinos, the pit boss may stop the action at a table so that security guards with clip boards can arrive to do a cash inventory.

TALL ORGANIZATION - organization that has numerous hierarchical levels and narrow spans of control.

TAP-OUT - lose one's total bank or money.

TAPPERS - dice with an inside shifting weight.

TARGET MARKET - a large, easily identifiable, and accessible group of people who have common interests so that a company can sell to them.

TARIFF - published fares, rates, charges, and/or related conditions.

TASK FORCE - temporary joining of personnel from different organizational subunits to accomplish a specific, well-defined complex task.

TASK SIGNIFICANCE - the degree to which the job has an important impact on the organization.

TAT - con game using dice with only high numbers.

TEAR UP - pretending to tear up a check from a mark and then cashing it.

TECHNICAL SKILL - specific knowledge of and ability to perform specific tasks and duties.

TECHNOLOGY - major techniques or tasks performed to produce the output of an organization.

TELEGRAPH - nonverbal action that betrays intentions to others, like security.

TELL - in poker, a nervous reaction by a player that signals his cards.

TELLAS CONSENT DECREE - in 1981, the EEOC won a discrimination suit against twenty Las Vegas hotels, which opened dealer opportunities to women and minorities, resulting in the setting of hiring quotas.

TEN RICH - high number of ten count cards remaining in the deck according to a card counter.

TERMINAL - the keyboard and monitor for a computer system.

THEORETICAL HOLD - in slots, the intended hold percentage or win as computed by reference to its payout schedule and reel strip settings. Deviation of the actual hold percentage from the theoretical hold percentage can be an indication of problems.

THEORY X - traditional view of motivation that assumes employees must be closely supervised and controlled.

THEORY Y - theory of motivation that assumes employees are self motivated and can be relegated authority.

THEORY Z - motivation theory that suggests employees should be given a participatory role in defining their jobs and in decision making.

THERE'S WORK DOWN - crooked dice are being used.

THEY'RE BURNING UP - dice that make pass after pass.

THIN ONE - dime.

THIRD-BASE - 1) far left-hand seat on the blackjack table, 2) last hand dealt.

THIRD DOZEN - in roulette, a bet on the numbers twenty-five through thirty-six.

THREE-NUMBER BET - in roulette, a bet paying eleven to one.

THREE OF A KIND - in poker, three cards of the same number.

THREE-WAY CRAPS - in craps, when one player bets equal amounts on two, three, and twelve separately, yet concurrently.

THUMB-OUT - process of using the thumb of the hand, holding a stack, to equalize a series of stacks of cheques.

TIE - hand in which both the player and dealer hold the same total value.

TIE-UP - person who keeps the mark interested in the scam until the end.

TIGHT - 1) very little known cheating technique, 2) hustler who can keep a secret.

TIGHTWAD - miserly or stingy person.

TIME-AND-A-HALF - 1) when a player has blackjack, dealer pays one and one half times the bet, 2) overtime pay.

TIME AND MOTION STUDY - process of analyzing jobs to determine the best movements for performing each task. For example, watching dealers to eliminate any superfluous moves so that play can be faster.

TIME MANAGEMENT - scheduling time effectively.

TIP - to reveal cheating secrets.

TITLE VII - in employment, the portion of the 1964 Civil Rights Act that prohibits discrimination in hiring and promoting.

TOILET - term for casino.

TOKES - tips, gratuity.

TOKE-BOX - a slotted, locked box for tips.

TOKE SPLIT - pooling and distributing all tips to all dealers.

TOM - player who leaves little or no tip.

TOOLS - altered dice that cheaters use.

TOP - upper level management or reputable information source.

TOPS - a die that has duplicate numbers.

TOPPING THE DECK - cheater who palms off the top of the deck on the cut.

TOTAL QUALITY MANAGEMENT or TQM - philosophy of management that is driven by customer needs and expectations.

TOUCH - 1) ask for a loan, 2) money obtained by cheating.

TOURNEUR - in European roulette, the dealer who spins the wheel and throws the ball into the wheel runway.

TOUR OPERATOR - company that specializes in the planning and operation of prepaid, preplanned vacations.

TOUR ORGANIZER - individual who organizes tours for special groups of people.

TOUR PACKAGE - travel plan that includes elements of a vacation like transportation and accommodations.

TOUR WHOLESALER - company that plans, markets, and operates tours to intermediaries but rarely to the end user.

TOUR-BASING FARE - special reduced, round trip fare with date and time restrictions.

TOURISM - industry that caters to travelers that includes travel, hotels, transportation, etc.

TOUT - 1) ask for bets, 2) verbally promote a game.

TRAINING - learning process whereby people acquire skills, or knowledge to aid in the achievement of goals.

TRANSVERSALE PLEIN - in roulette, a three number bet on a horizontal row.

TRAP - bet that is not what it appears to be.

TRAY - in casinos, a specific area for handling chips.

TREY - in craps, three on a die.

TRIM - to defraud someone.

TRIP DICE - trimmed edges on a pair of dice.

TRIP WORK - altered dice that have some edges extended slightly to prevent them from rolling over those edges.

TRUE-COUNT - running count adjusted for the number of cards or decks remaining to be played.

TRY-OUT - interview audition dealing in front of supervisors.

TUB - wheel.

TUMBLE - discover a scam.

TURKEY - 1) ignorant blackjack player, 2) any unpleasant player to deal to.

TURN A SUCKER - convince a mark to help con others.

TURNOVER - process of employees leaving an organization and being replaced.

TWENTY-ONE - alternate name for blackjack.

TWINKLE - hidden mirror that allows dealer to see the cards as he deals.

TWO BITS - twenty-five cents.

TWOFER - in blackjack, $2.50 chip.

TWO NUMBER BET - in craps, a bet that one of two specific numbers will, or will not, be thrown before a seven.

TWO PAIRS - in poker, two cards of one value and two of another value.

TWO-ROLL BET - in craps, a bet decided by the next two throws.

TWO-WAY BET - bet between player and dealer where winnings are divided equally.

TYPE A BEHAVIOR - behavior marked by a chronic sense of time urgency and an excessive competitive drive.

TYPE B BEHAVIOR - behavior that is relaxed, easy going, and non-competitive.

-U-

UNCERTAINTY - situation where the decision maker does not have a clear probability estimate of the outcomes.

UNDERGROUND ECONOMY - unreported economic activity. For example, illegal gambling.

UNDER THE GUN - 1) in poker, a player who must bet first, 2) in card games, player to the left of the dealer.

UNEMPLOYMENT - 1) in economics, workers who would be willing to work at prevailing wages but cannot find jobs, 2) in the US Bureau of Labor Statistics, worker is unemployed, is not working and, either waiting for recall from layoff or has actively looked for work in the previous four weeks.

UNION - a formal association of workers that promotes the welfare of its members, such as the Teamster's Union.

UNIT - measure used by gamblers to set the size of their wagers, usually based on the minimum bet at a particular game.

UNPAID SHILL - steady low roller.

UP A TREE - dealer's face up card.

UPCARD - in blackjack, a dealer's card dealt face up.

UTILITY - in economics, the satisfaction derived from the consumption of a commodity.

-V-

VALIDITY - research term to reflect the extent to which differences in scores on the measurement reflect true differences among individuals, groups, or situations.

VALENCE - strength of the valuation of a reward.

VALUE-FOR-MONEY BET - bet where the true probability of a result is greater than the odds being offered against the result.

VARIABLE COSTS - expenses that change directly with sales volume.

VARIANCE - difference between expected and actual cash flow figures.

VELVET - winnings.

VERTICAL MARKETING SYSTEM - integration of all the levels of manufacturers, wholesalers, and/or retailers who cooperate to sell a product.

VIC - victim or mark.

VIGORISH - 1) a five percent commission charged by the house for certain bets, 2) house edge.

-W-

WALK - 1) player who leaves a gaming table, 2) the hotel turns away a guest due to a lack of rooms.

WALKED WITH - an expression referring to the amount of table cheques a player leaves the table with.

WALK-IN - a person who requests a room without a reservation.

WALKING ON HIS HEELS - dazed.

WANT - a felt need shaped by a person's knowledge, culture, and personality.

WASH - breaking even.

WASHING-THE-CARDS - combining several decks of cards prior to shuffling by mixing them together on the table in random fashion.

WAY BET - in keno, a ticket marked to combine number bets in various ways.

WAY OFF - defective.

WEED - palm or remove bills while handling money.

WEIGHT - cheater jargon for loaded dice.

WELL HEELED - sophisticated.

WELSH - fail to pay a gambling debt.

WELSHER - gambler who fails to pay off on his gambling losses.

WHALE - term used by casino employees to describe a big bettor. For example, a credit line in excess of $50,000.

WHEEL - roulette wheel or game.

WHEEL ROLLER - roulette dealer.

WHIP SHOT - a controlled dice shot in which the two dice are spun from the hand and strike the table surface with a flat spinning motion so that the controlled numbers are on top when the dice stop.

WHIP CUP - cheater's dice cup with inner surface polished.

WHIRL - bet covering seven and the horn numbers in five equal amounts.

WHISTLE BLOWING - employees who report fraudulent or wasteful organizational activities to appropriate authorities.

WHITE ON WHITE - marked cards with small white markings on white border.

WHITES - one dollar.

WIDE OPEN - a lot of fast moving game action.

WILD CARD - card(s) given the power to substitute for other cards in suit and value.

WIN - the amount of each dollar wagered that is won or held by the house before operating expenses and other costs have been paid and does not represent profit.

WINDFALL - an unexpected large influx of money.

WINDOW - a cheater's term for location where dealer's hole card can be seen.

WIRE - 1) sign used between players, 2) in slots, a device used to rig a payout, 3) secretly worn tape recorder.

WIRED - in blackjack, a good hand.

WIRE JOINT - corrupt gambling house where tables are rigged or dice are magnetized.

WIREMAN - in slots, a cheat who slips a wire into a drilled hole in the machine to control the spinning wheels.

WON'T BITE - will not take the risk.

WON'T SPRING - will not pay the bill for others.

WOOD - non-player.

WORK - 1) deformed dice, 2) process of changing the dice.

WORKFORCE DIVERSITY - employees in organizations are heterogeneous in terms of gender, race, ethnicity, or other characteristics.

WORKING BETS - in craps, all money or chips that are riding on the next roll of the dice.

WORK TEAMS - groups of individuals that cooperate in completing a set of tasks.

WORLD-CLASS SERVICE - level of service that stresses personal attention to each guest.

WORSE OF IT - disadvantage.

WRONG BETTOR - in craps, a player who bets against the shooter by placing the bet "don't come" or "don't pass".

-X-

-Y-

YARD - one hundred dollars.

-Z-

ZERO - the thirty-seventh number on a roulette wheel.

ZERO-BASE BUDGETING - system in which budget requests start from zero regardless of previous appropriations.

ZERO-OUT - settle the account in full.

ZOMBIE - gambler who betrays no outward emotion.

ZOOM - in security, a camera with the capacity to magnify the image.

ZUKES - gratuities, tips.